Daniel Cohen

Jesse Ventura
The Body, The Mouth, The Mind

Twenty-First Century Books
Brookfield, Connecticut

Front and back cover photographs courtesy of AP/Wide World
Photos, ©Mark Solomon/Corbis, ©Titan Sports/Sygma

Frontispiece courtesy of Walter Iooss, Jr./*Sports Illustrated*

Photographs in insert courtesy of ClassMates.Com Yearbook
Archives: p. 1 (all); www.corbis.com/Corbis: p. 2 (top); Zade
Rosenthal/Photofest; p. 2 (bottom); ©Mark Solomon/Corbis: p. 3;
©Duomo/Corbis: pp. 4 (top), 7 (bottom); ©Will Hart/Allsport: p. 4
(bottom); ©Titan Sports/Sygma: p. 5; Archive Photos: p. 8;
AP/Wide World Photos: pp.6 (both), 7 (both).

Library of Congress Cataloging-in-Publication Data
Cohen, Daniel, 1936-
Jesse Ventura : the body, the mouth, the mind / by Daniel Cohen.
p. cm.
Includes bibliographical references (p.) and index.
ISBN 0-7613-1905-0
  1. Ventura, Jesse—Juvenile literature. 2. Wrestlers—United
States—Biography—Juvenile literature. 3. Governors—Minnesota—
Biography—Juvenile literature. [1. Ventura, Jesse. 2. Wrestlers.
3. Governors.] I. Title.
GV11963.V46   C65 2001   977.6'053'092—dc21
[B]   2001016181

Published by Twenty-First Century Books
A Division of The Millbrook Press, Inc.
2 Old New Milford Road
Brookfield, Connecticut 06804
www.millbrookpress.com

Contents

Introduction

"If You Understand Pro Wrestling . . ."

An old wrestling fan buddy of mine used to say, "If you understand pro wrestling you'll understand America." It is one of those statements that sounds wise and profound until you realize you don't know what it means.

I didn't know what it meant until November 5, 1998, when I looked at the front page of *The New York Times* and saw that former wrestler Jesse "the Body" Ventura had been elected governor of Minnesota.

The Times didn't have to tell me who Jesse was. I knew who he was from his days as part-time wrestler and full-time announcer for the World Wrestling Federation (WWF). I followed his career when he moved over to World Championship Wrestling (WCW). But after that he seemed to have dropped out of wrestling, and off my screen, until that rather startling story in *The Times*.

I never saw Jesse wrestle in person. By the time he became popular, professional wrestling had become basically a cable television event. But I admit—with less shame than I once would have—that, yes, I am a wrestling fan. Have been since I was a boy—a long time ago. While I never saw Jesse wrestle in person, I did see his old adversary Verne Gagne wrestle at Marigold Gardens in Chicago many times.

Like Jesse I grew up in the Midwest—not the South Side of Minneapolis, but the South Side of Chicago. I went to high school with guys like Jesse. I knew their families. And suddenly I knew what my old buddy meant about understanding wrestling and understanding America.

So when the chance to write a biography of Jesse Ventura came up, I jumped at it. This big shaven-headed guy with his loud voice and outrageous opinions is not just an aberration or a freak. If you understand who he is, where he came from, and why he appeals to so many people—particularly young people—you will understand something about America.

Chapter One

The first, and most important, thing you have to know is that Jesse Ventura isn't his name. It's the name he wrestled under; it's the name he was elected governor of Minnesota under. It's the name that made him famous. But it isn't the name he was born with.

He was born in Minneapolis, Minnesota, on July 15, 1951. The name on his birth certificate was James George Janos. Everybody called him Jim.

The famous and colorful Jesse Ventura has never tried to deny that he was once the ordinary and obscure Jim Janos. Indeed, he is extremely proud not only of who he is but who he was.

His father's family came from the central European area long known as Czechoslovakia. When James once described himself as being a "Czech," his aunt angrily corrected him by telling him he was "Slovak!" She wanted him to know who he was and to be proud of it. The Czechs were the "city people," the Slovaks the "country people," according to his aunt.[1] Czechoslovakia has now been broken up into two tiny countries—one for Czechs and the other for Slovaks.

The Janos family originally settled in Pennsylvania and his grandfather worked in the coal mines. But his grandfather figured out that the mines were, in Jesse's word, "killers." And the family moved to Minnesota to find a better life.

On his mother's side the family name was Lenz. They were of German origin, but had also come to settle in the Midwest, in Iowa.

World War II and the Army brought George Janos and Bernice Lenz together. George had enlisted in the Army at the maximum age of thirty-six. He became a sergeant and served under the legendary "Blood and Guts" commander General George Patton in North Africa. Bernice outranked him. She was an army nurse and had reached the rank of first lieutenant. In later years, George Janos would occasionally needle his wife by calling her "the lieutenant" and wondering out loud what was wrong with "these officers."

Though both "the sergeant" and "the lieutenant" had served in North Africa, they didn't

actually meet until after the war, when they were introduced by a man who was described as "the colonel." They were married in 1946. This was no case of young love. George Janos was forty, his new wife ten years younger. George had little more than an elementary school education. Bernice, a hardworking and determined woman, had put herself through nursing school. The couple moved to south Minneapolis. It was a working-class area populated mostly by people of Scandinavian descent, so much so that it was often called "Swede Town." Bernice worked at a number of hospitals, finally becoming chief nurse anesthetist at North Memorial Medical Center. George became a laborer for the city streets department. They were a solid working-class, blue-collar couple.

Their first son, Jan, was born in 1948. Their second son, Jim—the future wrestler and governor—was born three years later. The two boys grew up big, strong, and athletic. But aside from that they were about as different as can be imagined. Jan was quiet, introspective, a diligent student, and very neat. Jim was, well, a real handful for his parents. Later, when he became a parent, he said that his own son had given him a lot less trouble than he had given his own parents. Jim Janos was a loudmouthed, troublemaking slob. Perhaps he wouldn't describe himself quite that way—but that's what it amounts to.

The Janos family was a very old-fashioned one. No matter how outrageously Jim might

sometimes behave, he was devoted to his parents, particularly his mother. Besides, at that time and in that place, a certain amount of what might be called "high spirits" was expected from boys, and it was tolerated up to a point. In family matters Jim had to be polite and respectful. And he usually was.

The Janos family was old-fashioned in other ways: They were hardworking and thrifty. Since they both worked they had a pretty good income for the time. But like many of her generation, Bernice Janos was haunted by memories of the Great Depression, when her family had known real poverty. She remembered plenty of meals where her large family had had nothing to eat but oatmeal, and sometimes nothing at all. Bernice was always careful with money, and would never buy anything on credit. If the family needed a new car they would wait until there was enough in the bank to pay for it, all at once and in cash. She was a determined, even stubborn woman—and it was she who really ran the family.

Jesse recalls only one act of financial exuberance on the part of his father. There are lots of lakes in Minnesota, and lots of Minnesotans have lakefront cottages. These are not fancy beach houses for the rich. They are simple, often downright primitive cottages, where families gather during summer vacations. George Janos badly wanted a cottage, and so he raided the family treasury for money to buy a piece of lakefront property. Then he waited for the

expected explosion from his frugal wife. Much to everyone's surprise she took it calmly, announcing only that they would have to make do with their old car for a while longer.[2]

The whole family—grandfather, cousins, and so on—pitched in to help build the cabin. Even the boys, who were still quite young, were allowed to move lumber and hammer in a few nails. Many of Jesse Ventura's happiest childhood memories are of days spent at the cabin on the lake. The family still owns it. The cabin is, he says, "a family legacy."

His memories of school are not quite as happy. He was at best an average student—not terribly interested in schoolwork. But he lit up when it came to sports—he loved sports.

One of the sports he loved best was professional wrestling. Back in the late 1950s and early 1960s pro wrestling wasn't the big glitzy spectacle it is today. It was much more of a local phenomenon. Different promoters controlled different geographical areas. There was a good deal of wrestling shown on early television, mainly because it was easy and cheap to broadcast. Matches were also broadcast on the radio, particularly in areas like Minnesota where it was extremely popular. Jan and Jim Janos were big wrestling fans. Jim learned the pro holds and moves, or at least he tried to. Sometimes he practiced on his friends in gym class.

Once an elementary schoolteacher asked her class what they wanted to be when they grew up. Jim Janos replied that he wanted to

be a professional wrestler. The teacher dismissed this as a "ridiculous idea" and told him to sit down. Another teacher, however, predicted that he would become a boxer and later a sports announcer. Not precisely on target, but not too far off either.

George Janos was, in most circumstances, a friendly and easygoing man. But there was one subject that always got him worked up—politics. Basically he was a working-class, labor union Democrat. But even more basically he disliked and distrusted all politicians and did not care much for the government in general. He didn't think that politicians were friends of the working man.

Jesse remembers dinners where the family sat around eating and watching the news on television. Sometimes his father would become so upset by what he saw that he would begin yelling at the TV. "He ranted and raved and carried on to the point where my mom was ready to toss him down to the basement."

He would corner unsuspecting guests and pour out his political opinions, usually angry and bitter ones. "George was a really, really nice guy. You could sit down and talk to him for hours about anything but politics," said George Ritter, an old family friend. "You never wanted to discuss politics with George."[3]

The particular object of George Janos's rage was Richard Nixon. During the Watergate scandal of the 1970s, George would become purple

with rage every time he saw Nixon on television. Jesse always figured that his dad's hatred of Nixon grew out of the fact that he once actually voted for him in 1960. As a good Democrat, George Janos would not normally have voted for Republican Nixon. But Nixon was running against John F. Kennedy, a Democrat who was also a Catholic. Jesse believes that his father voted for Nixon because, like many others at that time, he thought if a Catholic became president the pope would be running the country. George Janos apparently was never able to forgive himself for that misguided vote.[4]

George Janos, a deeply patriotic ex-military man, also opposed the war in Vietnam. He was not opposed to war in general—but there was something about that war that didn't seem right to him. He couldn't understand why the United States was there. "Somebody's makin' money," he would say. "Somebody's makin' money." And his son, who actually fought in Vietnam, echoes his father's view. "By God, I think he was right."

By the time Jim Janos got to Roosevelt High School, home of the Teddys, he was someone to be noticed. He was the biggest kid in his class. He was the biggest kid in all his classes. When he was a senior he was 6 feet 2 inches (188 centimeters) and a muscular 190 pounds (86 kilograms). He was voted "Best Physique" by his class. And just in case you still failed to notice him, he was also a flamboyant dresser.

One old friend recalls his "Errol Flynn shirt" with big puffy sleeves. "He enjoyed being the center of attention."

Jim Janos was an athlete, but not a wrestler. In high school Jim's specialty was swimming. Both he and his brother were captains of their high school swimming teams. This was a talent both boys inherited from their father, who was also an excellent swimmer.

In high school Jim still wasn't much of a student. But there was one class in which he took a lively interest—history. He wasn't one of those kids who sits back silently during class discussion. He had a loud voice and definite opinion about almost everything. He was very much George Janos's son.

Other political figures in the United States have admitted that they had a "wild youth" and then quickly go on to another subject—any other subject. Jesse Ventura says he had a wild youth and then goes on to supply the details. He talks about his circle of friends, the South Side Boys, as being "pretty wild kids."

Among the South Side Boys, drugs were not a big deal and they were not nearly as widely available as they were to become just a few years later—but there was plenty of hard and illegal drinking. In blue-collar neighborhoods, underage drinking by boys was pretty much winked at so long as it didn't get completely out of hand. It was part of growing up—a sign of manhood. Jesse admits that a lot of people died

before drunken driving began to be taken seriously, "as it should have been."

"We weren't juvenile delinquents: I wouldn't put it that way. We just had a streak of mischief in us." Like the night the South Side Boys made an effigy of a hated teacher and hung it from the school flagpole. When they were finished they took the ladder they had stolen to hang the effigy and threw it at a school window.

People who knew Jim Janos at school don't remember him as being a violent person, or a bully, though he was certainly big enough and loud enough to intimidate most of his classmates if he wanted to. He was just a big friendly guy who everybody wanted to pal around with. He had a lot of girlfriends but no one special. He just wanted to have fun.

Still, Jim wouldn't back off from an argument, or a fight, and there were plenty of them. There were no guns or knives, but Jim and his friends secretly made what they called "fist loads" in shop class. These were 4-inch-long (10-centimeter) pieces of pipe that you held in your fist when you hit someone. It was the sort of behavior that might get you arrested today, but not in the early 1960s and not in the neighborhood Jim Janos grew up in. "It was just part of life. You accepted it."

Chapter Two

The Janos family wanted their boys to go to college, get an education, and get good jobs. It was the American dream for this hard-working blue-collar family. Bernice Janos was particularly hopeful for Jim, who she always thought of as "the Son Who Would Go to College." It didn't quite work out that way, at least not at first.

When the boys graduated from high school the Vietnam War was still being fought. Many of the South Side Boys were being drafted, or had enlisted in the military. A young man could avoid the draft, or at least be able to put it off by going to college. But for boys growing up in

south Minneapolis, college was not an inevitable or obvious choice for lots of reasons, both social and economic.

Jim Janos had been trying for a swimming scholarship to Northern Illinois University. He was a good enough swimmer, but his grades, while far from disastrous—mostly Bs and Cs—were not good enough to earn him that scholarship, particularly since he was an out-of-state student.

It was the summer of 1969. Jim got himself a job with the highway department, but he was angry and bitter about missing out on the scholarship. And he was drifting. He didn't know what he was going to do with the rest of his life. He halfheartedly enrolled in a small state college.

By the summer of 1969 the war in Vietnam was beginning to go badly for Americans. It had originally been thought of as a little war that could be won quickly with relatively few American casualties. Now a lot of young Americans were coming back from Vietnam in boxes, and protests against the war were rising, particularly on college campuses. But there were few, if any, antiwar protests in blue-collar south Minneapolis. Though doubts about the wisdom and ability to win the war were rising, the young men in that area often didn't go to college. They just kept enlisting or getting drafted, and sometimes getting killed.

While George Janos did not believe that the United States should be fighting a war halfway

around the world for no apparent reason, he was also a thoroughly patriotic man. And as a proud World War II veteran, he would not think of trying to stop his sons from joining the military. As a thoroughly practical man, however, he didn't want his boys to wind up in the Army or the Marine Corps, where he didn't think they would learn anything that might be useful later in life. The Navy or Air Force were preferable. There you could learn skills that would land you a good job after you got out.[1]

In the summer of 1969 Jim Janos wasn't thinking about his future career. In fact, he wasn't thinking very far ahead at all. So when his best friend, Steve Nelson, told him that he was planning to try to enlist in the elite Navy unit called the SEALs, and he wanted Jim to come with him, Jim agreed.

This was not quite as unexpected or impulsive a decision as it may have seemed. Jim's brother Jan had joined the SEALs a few years earlier. Jan had first joined the Navy, and then signed up for the SEALs after seeing an old World War II movie called *The Frogmen*. Jan made it into the elite unit but he was no romantic about the SEALs or the military in general and had not pushed his kid brother to join up. Quite the opposite. "Don't join the service," he told Jim when he came home on leave after a particularly brutal stint in Vietnam. "Stay home. Go to college. Have fun. Don't get involved in this war."

Jim wasn't taking that kind of advice and with his buddy Steve went down to the recruiting station just to "talk." Here were two big, strong eighteen-year-olds who didn't know what they wanted to do with their lives meeting experienced military recruiters. It was no contest. "They're like car salesmen," the mature Jesse Ventura recalled. They were introduced to the Navy "buddy program," which guaranteed that they could go to boot camp together just to make signing up seem more attractive and friendly. And when the recruiters heard that the boys were interested in the SEALs, they just lit up. They flattered Jim and Steve by telling them they could be part of the elite, the best of the best, the toughest. How could two restless and aimless recent high school graduates resist?

By the time they walked out of the office they had enlisted in the U.S. Navy. "I didn't plan to enlist," Ventura later told an interviewer. "They're recruiters. That's their job. I got down there, signed on the line, and got the military ID."

The unit that eventually became the SEALs began during World War II. The original unit started with a group of sailors who were selected for the nearly suicidal task of clearing obstacles from the beaches of Normandy in preparation for the D-Day landings in 1944. Later in the war the group was expanded to do underwater demolition work in the Pacific.

Their exploits were celebrated in the 1951 film *The Frogmen*, which had inspired Jan Janos to enter the Navy. Underwater Demolition Teams (UDTs) were used during the Korean War, and later still in Vietnam.

It was President John F. Kennedy who officially created the SEALs. He wanted each branch of the military to create special teams, or special forces, that were to carry out clandestine, unconventional, and highly dangerous missions. The Navy created the SEAL (SEA-Air-Land) teams in 1962. They were drawn from the UDTs, but in addition to being trained in underwater demolition, they were also trained in counterguerrilla warfare, including, if necessary, assassinations. As if planting and disarming underwater explosives wasn't dangerous enough, these guys also had to go ashore and fight.

President Kennedy called them "the best of the best," and the SEALs rapidly acquired a romantic, fearsome, and almost legendary reputation that they carefully cultivated. Since their operations were often clandestine they undertook a lot of secret missions. It was hard to be quite sure what they did or did not do. That, of course, added to their mystique. It was the sort of unit that would appeal to eighteen-year-old Jim Janos, who prided himself on never backing down to anyone or anything and being able to overcome every physical obstacle.

Later, Jesse Ventura would write in his autobiography that another reason he wanted to try to join the SEALs was to overcome his fear of heights. Now you might think that if you wanted to overcome a fear of heights you would join the Air Force and not a program where you spent a lot of your time underwater in a frog-man suit. But SEALs also received training in shinning down ropes out of helicopters, and in parachute jumping. "You can't be too afraid of heights and jump out of airplanes!" Ventura believes in confronting fear and conquering it. "I don't like to be afraid."[2]

Jim and his friend took a deferred enlist-ment. That meant that they didn't actually have to report for 120 days. Jim spent a month making money at the highway department, and spent the rest of his time and all of his money having a good time.

On a freezing January 5, 1970, Jim Janos's mother drove him to the Federal Building in Minneapolis where he was to report. Steve was there too. They were shipped off to Navy boot camp in San Diego, California. There they found themselves standing in a barracks in the middle of the night with some little officer screaming abuse at them for no reason. Jim turned to his friend and said, "Steve, you're lucky if I don't kill you right now."

Navy boot camp was no great challenge to a couple of high school athletes like Jim and Steve. But getting through Navy boot camp does not automatically make you a SEAL; it is just the first step. You don't get to be "the best of the best" so easily. In fact, the vast majority of those who apply to become SEALs never even make it through SEAL basic training.

Jim Janos nearly didn't make it into SEALs basic training. SEAL recruits can't be color blind. Jim is color blind. And when he first took the eye test he flunked. Somehow, he managed to get past the test for color blindness when he took it a second time, though his color perception had not improved. The fact that his brother had already been a SEAL probably helped.

The first phase of SEAL training is basically to push the recruits as hard as possible both physically and mentally and see who is still standing at the end. Recruits are made to run through obstacle courses in combat boots and spend days slogging through the mud, just to see how they stand up to being wet and uncomfortable. They have to swim miles in the punishing Pacific surf and guide rubber rafts past sharp rocks in the pounding surf. All the time an officer is yelling at them, telling them how weak and worthless they are. Twenty years later Jesse Ventura, now a successful professional wrestler, met his first SEAL instructor at a reunion. The meeting made the hair on the back of his neck stand up. "That's how scary these guys are," said Ventura.

The five-week training culminates in what the instructors call Motivation Week and the trainees more accurately call Hell Week. It's doing everything you have been doing the past five weeks, but with practically no sleep at all.

At this point, Ventura admits, "quitting starts to look awful good."

Jim Janos was strong, tough, and an outstanding swimmer—but he just couldn't keep his mouth shut, so inevitably he became a special target for his instructors. During one of his slogs through the swamp Jim picked up a 3-inch-long (7-centimeter) mudfish. His instructor saw this and made him swallow it—whole.

Having an older brother who was already a SEAL was both an advantage and a disadvantage. Most of the instructors already knew your name. But you also had a reputation to live up to. In order to distinguish between the two Janos brothers they were given nicknames—almost titles. Jan was "Janos the Clean." Younger brother Jim was "Janos the Dirty." Ventura concedes that the titles were pretty accurate reflections of the differences between him and his brother.[3]

An average SEAL class starts with 100 to 120 recruits. Between 20 and 35 graduate. Jim's class was exceptional; 38 of them finished. Jim Janos was one of them.

The second phase of the SEAL training was demolition and land warfare. Basically, the recruits learned how to blow things up. Ventura is quick to point out that they weren't trained in the dangerous task of disarming bombs. That was the work of the EOD—Explosive Ordnance Division. They were trained only to build bombs and set them off. When in doubt, he recalls, just put in more explosives.

The third phase of the training was advanced underwater diving, mostly diving deeper and staying under longer. If you survive all of that you graduate. According to Ventura they give you a diploma, a nice ceremony, and you get to shake an admiral's hand.

And it still isn't over. Jim and his remaining buddies were shipped off to the Army Airborne School in Fort Benning, Georgia, for three weeks of parachute training. Because of his fear of heights this was in many ways the toughest part of his training.

After jump school there is what is called SERE school—Survival Escape Resistance and Evasion. That teaches you what to do and what not to do if you are ever captured. And then there are seven weeks of very realistic training operations.

SEAL training is not just rugged, it's dangerous and can be deadly. At one point it nearly killed Jim Janos. During one of the seven-week training operations, Jim was part of a team that was supposed to "blow up" a couple of bridges. It was night and the small boat he was in swept over a dam that no one in the SEAL crew knew was there. "I got a brief, crazy vision of myself as a cat in a cartoon, leaving claw marks all the way down."[4]

He was thrown into the swirling water, which was sucking him under. He had a lot of gear strapped to his body and he could do absolutely nothing to break free from the current. At that point he assumed that he was

going to die, and accepted that fact. But then his feet touched bottom and he was shot back to the surface. He should have died, but he didn't. "It made me think."

But to hear Jesse Ventura tell it now, the most dangerous part of the whole process was not the training itself, but the time off, when he and his SEAL buddies swaggered into tough border towns like Tijuana looking for trouble and usually finding it.

In 1998, Jesse Ventura told an interviewer, "I was never the same after training. Because you truly know who you are down inside . . . No matter what I do now, that is the scale, that is the measuring stick. And no matter what adversities I face in life, I always go back to training and I say, 'This is nothing compared to that.'"

After the training, Jim was shipped overseas and spent about a year and a half in Southeast Asia, part of the time in Vietnam. The war was beginning to wind down. The Americans no longer believed they could "win"; they were really looking for a dignified way out. But fighting was still going on.

And here the story of the career of Navy SEAL Jim Janos becomes just a bit murky. This most outrageously outspoken public figure simply refuses to talk about his Vietnam experiences. He insists that after he returned from his first tour of duty he and the other SEALs in his group were ordered by their commanding officer not to talk about what they had seen or done. He says he has obeyed that order for many years and will continue to do so.

Many years later, after he entered politics, Jesse Ventura relied heavily on his background as a SEAL to attract attention and enhance his reputation as a leader. He campaigned wearing a SEAL T-shirt. But when campaigning for office, a lot of politicians have fudged or exaggerated their military records. Because of his thoroughly uncharacteristic reticence about his combat career, some opponents insisted that he really didn't deserve the title of Navy SEAL. To really be a SEAL you have to take part in a certain number of combat missions, and there is no hard evidence that he ever took part in any actual combat missions at all at this late stage of the war.[5]

But there is no doubt that Jim Janos did serious and dangerous work in Vietnam, some of it in enemy territory. If he did not actually engage in combat it was not because he tried to avoid it. His military buddies and many of his previous SEAL instructors insist that any argument about whether or not he truly deserves the title Navy SEAL is a highly technical quibble and a highly unfair one. He did what he was trained to do and what he was ordered to do, and he did it all very well.

Chapter Three

On the Road

For all his talk about how much he loved being a Navy SEAL and how much fun he had being stationed in places like the Philippines, Jim Janos had absolutely no intention of reenlisting when his term was over. The Navy was offering substantial bonuses to keep well-trained people like Jim in the service, but he was having none of it.

As far as the SEALs were concerned the war was essentially over; they had nothing more to accomplish in Vietnam. By 1973 the war had not only become unpopular in America but most Americans considered the war either unwinnable, or the price of winning too high.

Almost everybody knew that it was only a matter of time before America pulled out of Vietnam completely. Public and private negotiations to end the war were going on all the time.

Even while he was still in the military, Jim Janos was participating in peace rallies in California. He was not there, he now admits, because he had developed an abhorrence for the war. He attended the rallies mainly because he found them a great place to meet women. The women of the peace movement, he said, looked upon him as a victim of the system who had been drafted to fight a terrible war that he now opposed. He never bothered to tell them that he had enlisted and then aggressively sought to become part of one of the special forces units with the most fearsome and bloodthirsty reputation, and that he was quite proud of that.

There was something else that Jim Janos became interested in as his term of service drew to a close—it was motorcycles and the life-style adopted by the motorcycle clubs. One of his SEAL buddies had first gotten him interested in riding Harley-Davidsons.

Jim began hanging around with a biker club, or "gang"—a word Ventura says gives the wrong impression—called the South Bay Mongols. He was initiated into the Mongols before he was actually discharged. He would ride into the base on his Harley wearing his Levi's and leather jacket with the Mongols' colors, or insignia, on the back. He would then put them

in his locker and don his neat navy uniform for the day. Before he left the base he would change back into his leather jacket and Levi jeans, the uniform of the biker, and ride off on his Harley.

His superior officers were somewhat concerned, but since Jim was due for discharge and had made it clear he didn't want to reenlist, there wasn't really anything they could do about it. He wasn't looking for a military career and he wasn't breaking any laws or regulations.[1]

The Mongols were southern California rivals to another and far-better-known outlaw biker gang, the Hell's Angels. The Mongols were mostly Mexicans. The president was James "Fatman" Rivera.

Some critics insist that Ventura has actually exaggerated his position with the Mongols and that he never really was a full-fledged member. They say he may have been a prospective member or just one of the many hundreds of wanna-bes who hung around at biker rallies. The critics say had he really been a Mongol he would have a tattoo on his shoulder that reads "Mongols Motorcycle Club." He doesn't have the tattoo. But in his autobiography Ventura says he was voted into the club as a full-fledged member and was actually third in command of his chapter.[2]

Ventura insists that the Mongols were not involved in serious criminal activity like the Angels. But in his unauthorized biography of Ventura, Jake Tapper says, "Many of the crew

was clearly involved in criminal activities, but according to law enforcement investigators, it was mostly small-time stuff—bar fights, dealing marijuana and methamphetamines, maybe the occasional possession of a firearm."

Jim Janos, however, was very careful not to get mixed up with the law, even in small ways. When he first began riding with the Mongols he was still in the military. Even a small infraction could get him involved not only with civilian law enforcement but with the military justice system as well. And that was much tougher. "I didn't break the law when I was a biker," he says. As is typical of Jesse Ventura's entire career, there is a lot of bluster about his biker days, but underneath it, there was a strong foundation of caution and good sense. He was not going to become an "outlaw."

Like many others, Jim Janos had become swept up in the biker mystique. Historically, there have been two high points for motorcycle gangs in America, one right after World War II, the other at the end of the Vietnam War. Newly discharged young men, just breaking free of military discipline and feeling out of place in the civilian world with no particular plan for their future, took to the open road.

That was Jim Janos. He was big, physically tough, and as a former SEAL not afraid of danger. He liked to drink hard, and party hard, and while he was not a lawbreaker by nature, he resented any restrictions on his freedom. "We

wanted to be left to ourselves," he says of the bikers.

He was also attracted by the flamboyant biker style. Jim, always the showman, always dying to be the center of attention, loved the biker outfit, the black leather jackets with the club insignia, the Levi's, the outrageous hairstyles, and, of course, the huge shiny and noisy Harleys. For a bunch of guys who insisted that all they really wanted was to be left alone, all of this was a magnet for attention. Maybe they wanted to be left alone, but they sure didn't want to be ignored. Whether deliberate or not, the biker projected an image of someone who was strange, powerful, and potentially violent and dangerous. It was someone you might want to leave alone, but someone you certainly had to notice.

And then there was "Janos the Dirty." In that way he fit right in. Ventura acknowledges that bikers were not the cleanest guys in the world. He was living in a rundown house strewn with motorcycle parts. He would use his bed sheets to wipe the oil off his hands. One of his proudest possessions was his "Originals." These were his first pair of Levi's. Once the biker puts them on, or so biker mythology states, he never washes them, no matter what. That is a point of pride. They are covered with oil stains that turn liquid again during hot weather. Ventura says he still has his "Originals," still unwashed, somewhere in his garage. One suspects that it would not take a bloodhound to locate them.

Jim Janos was discharged from active duty in December 1973, though he was still committed to two years in the reserves. He spent a few months riding and partying with the Mongols. But there was always a solid and practical core to the man. He looked around him and saw other bikers—some fifty years old who had nothing in life but their Harleys. The solid and practical side of Jim Janos didn't want that sort of a dead-end life. By the fall of 1974 he abandoned the bikers and southern California and returned to Minnesota, where he enrolled in college.

It was a good thing he got out when he did, because over the next few years the biker world of southern California turned a lot more violent. Open warfare had broken out between the Mongols and Hell's Angels, and a lot of Mongols and their associates were shot or otherwise killed by the Angels and vice versa.[3]

By the time this began, Jim was a student at North Hennepin Community College, a two-year school in Brooklyn Park, Minnesota. He was facing nothing more dangerous than freshman English. Jim didn't have much confidence in his academic abilities, or any clear idea of what courses he should take, but he turned out to be a better-than-average student. His English teacher remembers him as being a particularly good talker, funny, and despite his size and bluff manner, or perhaps because of them, he was "endearing."

Jim also joined the college's football team and harbored hopes of playing professional football someday. At the very least he hoped that his football would get him a scholarship to a university. That didn't work out. He was certainly big enough and strong enough for football, but he just couldn't take the game very seriously. He was twenty-two years old, had gone through the physical hell of SEALs training, had ridden with a motorcycle gang, and here were the coaches trying to tell him that each game was life or death. He had really faced death, and he knew the difference. Besides, Jim loved to showboat. After a tackle he would rip off his helmet and wave to the crowd. His coaches didn't appreciate that. Football is a team sport; Jim was not a team player.

Far more significant than football was acting. It was at North Hennepin that Jim Janos made his acting debut. The school was staging a production of the classic ancient Greek comedy *The Birds* by Aristophanes. The play, incidentally, is about political corruption in ancient Athens. The director was looking around for someone to play the part of Hercules. He saw Jim working out in the weight room and decided at once that he was the man for the part of the muscular Greek hero. When Jim was offered the part it was probably the first time in his life that he had ever heard of Aristophanes.

In early March 1975, Jim appeared in four sold-out performances of the play. He enjoyed the experience so much that he enrolled in a theater course. He wasn't really thinking of becoming an actor. But he did think the dramatic training might help him fulfill his childhood dream of becoming a professional wrestler. Jim had to financially support himself, and he found a way to use his intimidating physique and booming voice. He got a job three nights a week as a bouncer in a tough bar called The Rusty Nail.

It's important to take a look at Jim Janos at this moment in his life. He was now twenty-three years old, well over 6 feet (1.8 meters) tall, and nearly 200 pounds (91 kilograms). But there wasn't an ounce of fat on him. He was working out regularly and beginning to develop the physique that would later give him the most popular of his many nicknames, "the Body." As soon as he had been discharged from the Navy he let his hair grow until it reached his shoulders. And he dyed it blond. As usual you couldn't miss the guy.

Then one Tuesday night, "Ladies Night" at The Rusty Nail, nineteen-year-old Terry Masters showed up at the bar. At that time eighteen was the legal drinking age in Minnesota. One of the off-duty policemen who was also working the door checked her ID. She was one of the most beautiful girls Jim Janos had ever seen. He had to meet her, but for one of the very few

times in his life the talkative Jim didn't know what to say. So he asked to see her ID.

Terry pointed to the policeman and replied, "But I just showed it to him."

"I don't want to know how old you are," Jim said. "I just want to know your name."

Very slowly, and very deliberately, the young woman went through her purse, found her ID, and handed it to him. Her name was Terry Masters. She had just graduated from St. Louis Park High School. She was living with her uncle in Minnetonka, Minnesota, and doing secretarial work.

Later that evening the two sat down and talked. She said, "God! You look just like 'Superstar' Billy Graham!"

"I ought to," Jim lied, "he's my older brother."

That marked the beginning of a beautiful friendship.

Chapter Four

Minor Leagues and Marriage

"Superstar" Billy Graham, the name that brought Jim and Terry together, was an extremely popular professional wrestler of the 1970s. He was big, blond, and very muscular—he had once held the body-building title of Mr. Teenage America. He was also a strutting, preening, loudmouthed villain who broke all the rules in order to win—or, in wrestling parlance, a "heel." That was in opposition to the "babyface," or more popularly "face," a good guy who always followed the rules, was modest, and generally more normal looking than his "heel" opponent. In the 1970s the professional wrestling world was divided into "heels" and "faces."[1]

In professional wrestling today practically all the wrestlers are "personalities." They are all loudmouthed, arrogant, bizarre looking, and never follow the rules. There are no real "heels" and "faces" anymore. But in the 1970s, almost every match was a clear contest between "good" and "evil." The babyfaces usually won the match. Evil, arrogance, and obvious rule-breaking were not supposed to triumph. For the wrestling fan, however, evil was often more popular. The heels were a lot more fun to watch. And for wrestling fans, mostly teenage boys and young men, the heel also had the appeal of the outlaw, or the rebel, the guy who could dress as he wished, talk as he wished, and just thumb his nose at the rest of the world.

Jim Janos had grown up watching wrestling on television and listening to matches on the radio. He had seen "Superstar" Billy Graham wrestle in Minnesota. It wasn't so much Graham's prowess in the ring that impressed Jim. It was his effect on the crowd. He insulted them and they hated him for that, but he had them in the palm of his hand. When the Superstar wrestled, all eyes were on him. Jim later recalled thinking, "That's what I wanna do."

While he was "wrestling" with English at North Hennepin Community College he was also learning the tricks of the wrestling trade at the old Seventh Street Gym in Minneapolis. The gym was co-owned by an ex-professional wrestler named Eddie Sharkey. Sharkey remembers his old pupil affectionately. "The thing I liked about him most was his sense of humor. And he's the most honest man I ever met in my life. The old Seventh Street Gym had every crook in the world; he stood out as an honest man."

Professional wrestling has always gone through cycles of popularity in the United States. It was enormously popular in the 1920s, but popularity fell off during the Great Depression and World War II. During the 1950s it came back big on early television. But in the early 1970s popularity was once again at a low point in the cycle, except in places like Minnesota, where wrestling matches were still shown on TV every Saturday night and wrestlers like "Superstar" Billy Graham could pack a large arena.

Jim Janos was now seriously preparing for a career as a professional wrestler. He had already built up his body through intensive weight training, and he was downing handfuls of vitamins and a dozen raw eggs a day. Here was a man who clearly feared neither cholesterol nor salmonella in his drive for a more perfect body. A well-conditioned athlete already, he had the strength and endurance to be a wrestler. Sharkey was teaching him the moves—how to fall, how to protect himself, and how to protect his opponent. One of the cardi-

nal rules of professional wrestling was you can beat the other guy, but you're not supposed to do him serious injury. Sometimes it happens, but it's not supposed to. The next time it could be you. Sharkey recalls that Jim Janos was an easy guy to train because he was a lot smarter than most of the other wrestlers, and a lot more disciplined.

While Jim had "Superstar" Billy Graham as a role model and idol, Terry hated him. He was, after all, a heel. People were supposed to hate him. But Terry knew who he was and that was all Jim needed. The muscular bleached blond and the slim brunette hit it off famously right from the start. Actually, Jim Janos, who had always bragged about how attractive he was to women, was having a hard time getting dates since he moved back to Minnesota. He was uncharacteristically quite nervous.

Their first date was memorable if not romantic. Jim took Terry to a neighborhood bar, a place where he felt comfortable. He had gone there often with his friends; his father had even gone there. They were in the bar for about fifteen minutes when the police rushed in and grabbed some guy off a barstool. When he resisted the cops beat him up. The guy had been roughing up his girlfriend in the parking lot.

And they had different tastes in entertainment. She wanted to see the film *Love Story* with Ryan O'Neal. He took her to see *Death Wish* with Charles Bronson. Still, their relationship blossomed.[2]

The year 1975 was a big one for another reason. It was the year that Jim Janos became a professional wrestler, and became known as Jesse Ventura.

The name Jim Janos was too ordinary; it just wouldn't do in the theatrical world of pro wrestling. He needed something flashier. He always liked the name Jesse. As for Ventura, he got that one off the map—it's a small city on the beach north of Los Angeles. It fit the image of the blond surfer bad-boy that he was trying to cultivate. He would be Jesse Ventura "the Surfer." And he would be a heel. Everybody in the Midwest disliked blond surfers and beach bums from California.

In 1975 professional wrestling was still fragmented into local territories, each under the control of a different promoter. There were approximately twenty-four distinct wrestling organizations in the United States. Most of them were small and booked matches in Masonic halls and high school gymnasiums.[3]

The Minnesota area was the territory of the American Wrestling Alliance (AWA), which was controlled by promoter and former wrestling champ Verne Gagne. Because of the continuing popularity of wrestling in that part of the country it was one of the largest and most prosperous of the many wrestling associations, and it was far too big for the newly minted Jesse Ventura "the Surfer" to start his career. He would need seasoning in the minor leagues of wrestling.

Sharkey used his contacts and got Jesse—for we can now properly call him that—fixed up with the National Wrestling Alliance, which toured small venues throughout Missouri and Kansas. This was definitely the minor leagues of wrestling, but it was a place to start. Jesse jumped into his beat-up old Chevy and drove to Kansas City.

His first professional wrestling match was at an arena in Wichita. He was the bad guy, against veteran good guy Omar Atlas. Jesse lost, but it was a good loss and he remembers that first match fondly.

Back in the 1970s wrestling fans still seriously discussed the subject of whether wrestling was "fake." The standard answer from wrestlers like Jesse Ventura was to threaten to bodyslam you, and see if that was fake. Of course professional wrestling was, and is, fake in the sense in which the word is normally used. But the wrestlers do have a point, of sorts, in defending their sport. While the outcome of the match is predetermined, the action is not. And while it is not nearly as violent, painful, and dangerous as it looks, there really is a lot of pain and professional wrestlers are hurt regularly, and often seriously.

Before Jesse's first match, promoter Bob Geigel told him, "You know, kid, nobody wins their first match." Jesse knew.

It was up to the veteran Atlas to "call" the match. It all depended on crowd reaction. If the crowd was getting bored and restless, Atlas was

to deliver a couple of drop kicks and pin Ventura for a quick finish. If the crowd was yelling and screaming for more the match could go on longer, and Jesse would be allowed to throw Atlas out of the ring over the top rope. In those days throwing your opponent over the top rope was an automatic disqualification. You lost the match, but it was a showy way to go out, a lot better than just being pinned.

Jesse was Jesse, right from the start. He swaggered down to the ring shouting insults at the crowd, pounding his chest and telling everyone in his very loud voice just how wonderful and good looking he was and what ugly losers they were. The crowd hated him. And that was just great. In the wrestling world, the fans may have loved the babyfaces, but it was the heels who got them up on their feet and fired up their emotions. It was the heels who really brought in the crowds, and the promoters knew it. So did Jesse Ventura.

The match went well. The fans screamed and booed every time Jesse pulled a dirty trick, and cheered like mad every time he hit the canvas. At the finale Jesse and Omar faced one another in the middle of the ring. Omar whispered, "Amigo, throw me out over the top." He did. Omar landed with a thud and played hurt, and that stirred up the crowd even more. Jesse was disqualified, but he shouted that he had been "robbed" and strutted anyway. It was a big finish.

But the life of a minor-league professional wrestler was far from a glamorous or well-pay-

ing one. Jesse traveled constantly, driving from one small town to the next in his beat-up old car. Wrestling night after night, but never getting more than $65 a match and often a lot less. Wrestling promoters were notoriously cheap, when they were not downright crooked. They were the direct descendants of the carnival pitchmen.

One story often repeated in wrestling circles was about a Texas judge who had been called in to resolve a dispute between two Texas promoters. The judge delivered his report to a group of promoters, and it was obvious that he had resolved the dispute in a way that would fatten his own fee. At the end of the report one promoter stood up and said, "Well, this guy looks like the type who'd steal a hot stove and come back the next day for the lid, so I suppose he'll fit right in with us."[4]

Jesse had already begun his wrestling career before he got married. The hardest thing for him about his new career was that he missed Terry. At one point she came to visit him in Kansas City. He was living in a $23-a-week hotel—flophouse would probably be a more accurate description. That really didn't bother "Janos the Dirty." He had lived in worse places. But when Terry saw it she broke down and cried.

Jesse wanted to be with her and asked her to come down and live with him. She was having none of that. She wasn't just going to be his girlfriend and follow him from one crummy

location to another. Faced with the possible loss of the girl he loved, Jesse Ventura, who had never thought seriously about marriage, asked if she would marry him. She would.

Jim actually delayed the marriage a bit. The men in his family always married late, when they married at all. He had promised himself that he would not get married before he was twenty-four.

Jim and Terry were married on July 18, 1975—three days after his twenty-fourth birthday. Terry's mother was still trying to talk her out of the wedding, practically up to the moment she walked down the aisle.

The marriage took place at Timothy Lutheran Church in Saint Louis Park, a suburb of Minnesota. Terry made all the arrangements. One of the wedding pictures shows Jim with his shoulder-length bleached hair, his huge frame crammed uncomfortably into a tuxedo, grinning at the camera and looking frankly ridiculous.

Despite the difficulties and genuine hardships of minor-league wrestling, Jesse Ventura stuck it out. And he began to build a reputation, even if he was barely making a living. After a few months in Kansas his old mentor and coach Sharkey told him to move on to Oregon and the Pacific Northwest, where wrestling was more popular and it was often televised.

That move was Jesse Ventura's breakthrough.

Chapter Five

The Body

When Jesse Ventura arrived in Oregon he was still working on his "persona," his wrestling character. For a while he called himself "The Great Ventura," and he wore a mask. "To hide my good looks," he insisted. Unmasking him became a regular feature of his appearances.

In 1978 one of the wrestling announcers, taking note of Jesse's always-impressive physique, began calling him "the Body." It was a name that stuck. No more "Surfer," no more "Great Ventura," no more masks.

Jesse was a fanatic bodybuilder who exercised all the time, but he admits that at least some of his sculpted physique was due to the use of anabolic steroids. Steroids were legal and the dangers were not fully recognized in the mid-1970s. Most pro wrestlers (and a lot of other athletes) used them in quantity. Jesse Ventura's own idol, "Superstar" Billy Graham, was one of the early bodybuilder wrestlers and a heavy steroid user. Ultimately that ruined his career and his health.

The steroids affected Graham's joints to the point where even ordinary activities like getting out of a chair became painful, and the strain of wrestling became impossible. This was a lesson that was not lost on most later wrestlers, including Jesse Ventura. While steroids are still a part of the world of professional wrestling, they are not nearly as common as they once were.[1]

Jesse "the Body" began wearing brightly colored tights, enormous and ornate sunglasses, long earrings, a jewel in his deeply cleft chin, and what was to become a trademark for him, a feather boa. He still grew his hair long and dyed it blond, or for contrast sometimes green or purple. He now often wore a bandanna on his head to cover a growing bald spot. Face hair was usually some sort of small beard and a Fu Manchu mustache. Maybe he wasn't the most bizarre-looking character in the ring in those days, but he was right up there among the oddest.

What sort of wrestler was Jesse "the Body?" Most longtime wrestling fans would say that he wasn't very good at all. He was strong but

clumsy. He had a great physique, and he spent a lot of time posing and showing off his muscles. Sometimes he would stop right in the middle of a match to flex his muscles. That generally resulted in his opponent sneaking up behind him and knocking him to the mat, much to the delight of the crowd. But in pro wrestling, wrestling skills counted less and less. What sold the tickets were muscles and personality, and Jesse had plenty of both.

One of his most popular gimmicks was to strike a pose in the ring and then shout, "Take a look at this body, all you women out there—then look at the fat guy next to you eating pretzels and drinking beer. Who would you really rather be with?"[2]

He was a master at working up a crowd and he gave a great interview. That meant a lot in Oregon, where Saturday night wrestling was still a big TV draw and interviewing the wrestlers was part of every show.

The wrestling interview is an art form all its own. The announcer, usually a small and inoffensive looking individual, stands next to a tall, hugely muscled, very angry man. The wrestler shouts defiance into the microphone, insults the city where the match is being held, and threatens to pound his next opponent, the announcer, and anyone else he can think of, into jelly.

Jesse's raspy baritone was perfect for such a performance. And he was a natural born loudmouth, with a quick wit and a flair for the dramatic. Jesse says that he had a real talent

for irritating people. Veteran wrestling announcer Mean Gene Okerlund said that Jesse was a delight to interview because he actually had a brain; he kept up on current affairs and popular culture. "I'd just ask him a few questions and he'd roll."[3]

Jesse had something else that made him successful as a professional wrestler—discipline. The life of a pro wrestler is a nomadic one. They travel relentlessly from town to town, stay in hotels, and are faced with long hours of boredom between matches. A lot of the wrestlers spent their time on the road drinking and getting into trouble. Anyone who travels a lot on the job faces the same hazards when cut loose from home, family, and familiar surroundings. A lot of wrestlers couldn't handle the life. They became alcoholics or drug addicts.

But Jesse didn't go out drinking with the boys. He would work out in a gym when he could find one, or stay in the hotel researching the town he was in (so he could insult the people more effectively before his match) and watching soap operas on television. *The Young and the Restless* was his favorite. The scenarios in wrestling, with their stark confrontations between good and evil, have often been called soap opera for men.

And he called Terry every night. The loudmouthed villain with the feather boa was really a good family man. If the fans had known that, it probably would have killed his career.

Sometimes riling up the fans could be dangerous. He got a lot of death threats, but they amounted to nothing, just somebody blowing off steam at the "villain." However, he vividly recalls a night in Eugene, Oregon. After the match, he was being escorted back to the dressing room by the police. The heels always got a police escort to protect them from overwrought fans. But a fight broke out at ringside and the police had to take care of that first. With the focus of attention elsewhere, Jesse figured he was safe—when he was suddenly confronted by a teenager "with a wild look in his eye."

Jesse recognized him as someone he had told to shut up, probably more colorfully than that, earlier in the evening. Now the kid was coming for him and waving a dangerous-looking 10-inch (25-centimeter) hunting knife. Jesse was sure he was serious. The ex-SEAL knew he could take the kid down, but he was standing there in his tights. He didn't even have a towel to defend himself with. He figured he would probably be badly cut up before he got the knife. Fortunately, an off-duty cop who had taken his own kid to the matches saw what was happening, sneaked up behind the knife-wielding teenager, and slapped handcuffs on him before anyone got hurt.[4]

Jesse wasn't injured that time, but another time he *was* hurt by a seventy-year-old woman who dug her long fingernails into his back. "I didn't deck her, but I did tell the cops to arrest her."

You couldn't find Jesse Ventura's name in any phone book. As far as the telephone company was concerned, he was still Jim Janos. And he kept it that way for a long time. He did not want any angry nuts calling up and bothering his wife, and he didn't want any to come looking for him where he lived. He tried hard to keep his professional life and private life separate.

Role changes were, and still are, a common feature of pro wrestling. The good guy becomes a bad guy and vice versa. So after a while even the big-mouthed heel Jesse Ventura became a babyface. He was wrestling Buddy Rose, a long-time Northwest bad guy. A feud between the two had been hyped and wound up in a "Loser Leaves Town" match, another regular pro-wrestling gimmick. Ventura lost, and he left town. He went all the way back to Minnesota, where he joined up with Verne Gagne's AWA. He was still on the road a lot, but closer to home now, and that was important. In 1979, Jesse and Terry had their first child, a boy they named Tyrel. Jesse got the name from a book by one of his favorite authors, Western writer Louis L'Amour.

Gagne, who had been a superb technical wrestler in his own time, didn't have much respect for Jesse's wrestling skills. But Gagne the businessman, who wanted to put people in the seats, had a lot of respect for Jesse's ability to irritate people. Once again "the Body" became a heel.

Gagne teamed Jesse with Adrian "Golden Boy" Adonis. Together they became one of the AWA's chief draws. Adonis, who was the better wrestler, did most of the wrestling. Jesse, who was the better talker, did almost all the talking.[5]

To say that Jesse Ventura and Verne Gagne didn't get along would be to put the matter as mildly as possible. They loathed one another. They argued constantly, mostly about money. Gagne was one of those old-fashioned promoters who believed that wrestlers should be paid as little as possible. Ventura naturally believed they should be paid a lot more. Jesse was now making more money than he had ever made in his life, but with Gagne he could never tell what his next paycheck would be. That was entirely up to the whim of the promoter.

Despite the friction, Jesse's time in the AWA may have been the happiest and most satisfying in his wrestling career. He really loved his native state of Minnesota, and he was a star in his home territory. In 1980 he was one of the main attractions at a sold-out event at the St. Paul Civic Center. When he entered the ring the audience spent a full five minutes screaming obscenities at him while he posed and flexed. "It was very thrilling. I literally had that crowd in the palm of my hand."

It was still a time in professional wrestling history when there were twenty-four or so independent territories that more or less cooperated with one another. Sometimes if a wrestler stayed in one territory too long the fans would begin to get bored with him. So the promoters would make up an excuse to let a wrestler go to another territory for a time. That was the reason behind the "Loser Leaves Town" match that allowed Jesse to go back to the Midwest.

In January 1981, Gagne announced that Jesse had been suspended from the AWA for "outrageous behavior"—impossible since there was no behavior in professional wrestling that was considered too outrageous. What really happened is that the biggest promoter in the country wanted Jesse to wrestle in his territory for six months. In the spirit of the wary cooperation that then existed between the various wrestling organizations, Gagne allowed Jesse to go, but of course this could not be admitted publicly, hence the "suspension."

The promoter who wanted Jesse's services was Vince McMahon Sr., head of Capitol Wrestling Corporation (CWC). CWC had started in the Washington, DC, area but now was based in New York, and essentially controlled wrestling throughout the heavily populated Northeast. Jesse headed east and found Vince Sr. to be a really nice guy, a rarity among wrestling promoters. Jesse got a chance to wrestle some of the biggest names in the business, and he was so popular that Vince Sr. even sent him to Japan (where American-style professional wrestling has always been popular) for a match. Jesse was now making real money in the ring.

But by July 1981 his six months in the CWC was up, and it was back to Minnesota and shouting matches with Gagne—as usual over money. Jesse also began running Jesse's Gym, which was for weight lifters and bodybuilders rather than professional wrestlers. It was a way of assuring at least a bit of financial security to cushion him and his family from the capricious AWA promoter.

Money and security became an increasing concern for Jesse Ventura, not just because he wanted them but because he now needed them. In 1983, Jesse and Terry had their second child, a daughter they named Jade. From the moment she was born, Jade began having seizures, and for a while it looked as if she would never be able to lead a normal life, or possibly even survive. But after a long series of exhaustive and expensive tests the baby was found to have been born with a rare form of epilepsy. The condition was not curable, but it could, with difficulty, be controlled.

Jade spent sixty days in the hospital in intensive care. And, despite the fact that Jesse was making pretty good money wrestling and running his gym, the costs piled up. Professional wrestlers didn't have health insurance plans or any other benefits for that matter. His own private health insurance didn't come close to covering the costs. He was falling into debt, something his mother taught him he should never do.

Jesse needed money, so he made a big move. He defected from the Midwestern AWA and went to the newly formed World Wrestling Federation (WWF), and into a whole new world of professional wrestling.

Chapter Six

The Mouth

The man who changed the face of professional wrestling and, inadvertently, did more than anyone else to promote the future career of Jesse Ventura to national prominence was Vince McMahon Jr., son of veteran wrestling promoter Vince Sr.

Vince Jr. took over for his ailing father in the late 1970s and changed the name of the organization to World Wrestling Federation (WWF). Vince Jr. refused to recognize the old system, in which the country was carved up into a couple of dozen territories each controlled by a single promoter who more or less cooperated with the other promoters. He wanted it all. And the method he chose to get it all was cable television.

Vince Jr. realized that wrestling was not yet popular enough to gain a foothold in national broadcast television. But he also saw the growing power of cable television. New cable channels were springing up all over the country almost daily, and they were hungry for cheap, popular programming. Vince Jr. began taping his wrestling shows and selling them to cable channels all over the country, without regard to the old gentlemen's agreement about not directly competing with other promoters.

Pretty soon the fans were watching WWF shows on TV instead of going to the matches put on by local promoters. WWF stars became national rather than regional stars. There had been nothing like this since the early days of broadcast television in the 1950s, when wrestlers like Gorgeous George were household names across America.[1]

It was also Vince Jr. who broke the code of silence on the subject of whether wrestling was "fake" or not. He admitted that it was, though he didn't use the word "fake." It was not a sudden attack of honesty that made him do this. So long as wrestling was regarded, at least officially, as a legitimate sport, a measure of control was exercised by state athletic commissions, which oversaw sporting events in their state. It was a ridiculous situation because everybody in the athletic commissions knew that wrestling was

not a real sport. But pretending it was meant that the WWF, which had gone national, had to deal with athletic commissions in dozens of different states. To simplify matters Vince Jr. called his product "sports entertainment."

This move caused great consternation and real fear among many in the wrestling world. Promoters were afraid that once fans knew for sure that wrestling wasn't "real" they would lose interest. But Vince Jr.'s gamble paid off. The fans were not alienated or surprised. Calling it sports entertainment merely confirmed what most fans already knew and accepted. New fans were even relieved that the violence they saw wasn't as real as it looked. Professional wrestling became more popular than ever. Real or unreal, what wrestling fans wanted was a good show.[2]

Vince Jr. also began hiring away the top attractions from other promoters. One of those was Jesse "the Body" Ventura. He phoned Jesse in 1984 and asked him to come and work for the WWF.

At that moment, Jesse and Terry, good and responsible parents, were struggling with the problems and wrenching anxiety of having a seriously ill child. And Jesse was, as usual, fighting with Verne Gagne, who he felt wasn't being at all sympathetic to his family situation.

Jesse was making good money with the AWA, but there was no security and he really detested Gagne. Vince Jr. held out the promise of more money and more freedom. But there was a big risk. At the time nobody, including Vince Jr. himself, knew whether the bold gamble would succeed. He exuded confidence, but later confessed that at points the WWF was near collapse. If Jesse defected to the WWF, and the venture failed, his wrestling career would be finished. Neither Gagne, nor any of the other local promoters, would ever hire him again. But Jesse was ready to take the chance. He told Vince Jr. that he would have to give Gagne the usual thirty days notice before he quit.

"Why?" said Vince Jr. "You're never going to work for him again."

Then Jesse said that he would go in and have it out with Verne Gagne. "Why do that?" said Vince Jr. "Send him a telegram." And that's what Jesse did.

Years later, when Jesse got into a legal dispute with Vince Jr., Verne Gagne testified in court for Jesse. He was one of Jesse's strongest witnesses. Though he hated Jesse Ventura, he hated Vince McMahon Jr. even more.

Vince McMahon Jr.'s gamble paid off, and so did Jesse Ventura's. The new WWF raised wrestling to new heights of popularity and profitability. Jesse Ventura was one of its stars and riding the wave. In many ways he became a model for pro-wrestling stars of the future—pumped-up bodies, absolutely outlandish costumes and personalities, and better talkers and screamers than they were

wrestlers. More than ever they resembled comic-book characters.

Jesse was again teamed up with his old tag-team partner Adrian Adonis, and the team was managed by Classy Freddie Blassie. Blassie had a reputation as one of the meanest wrestlers, and when he retired he had the reputation of being one of the meanest managers. Blassie never liked Jesse and never hesitated to say so. He said Jesse always thought he was too smart to listen to anyone else. Later in his career others expressed the same opinion of Jesse Ventura.[3]

Meanwhile, Jesse was becoming a national star, not only as part of his tag team with Adonis, which was called the East-West Connection (Jesse was West, even though he came from Minnesota), but also as an individual wrestler. In the mid-1980s, he was featured in respectable publications like *People* magazine and *Sports Illustrated.* Jesse has said that the high point of his wrestling career came when he wrestled WWF champ Bob Backlund for the title in Madison Square Garden three times in a row. The place was sold out three times. "Selling out three times in the mecca of ring sports. I don't know how I could have topped that," Jesse wrote.

Backlund was the last of the real babyface wrestling champs. He was also a real wrestler, having won amateur championships. He was expected to retain his WWF championship in his matches with Jesse—and he did. He would have beaten Jesse even if the match had not been scripted. Much later Backlund imitated Jesse and went into politics.

Jesse Ventura wasn't the only star of this new era in wrestling, and he wasn't the biggest star either. That honor belonged to Terry Bolla, a name you may not recognize. But you will certainly recognize his wrestling name, Hulk Hogan. That name was chosen at a time when the Marvel Comics character The Incredible Hulk was also a popular television series. Another popular TV series of the time was *Hogan's Heroes*. At first Hulk Hogan dyed his hair red and was promoted as an Irish wrestler. But soon he switched to shoulder-length bleached-blond hair in the "Superstar" Billy Graham mode, and became another California surfer. Unlike Jim Janos, Terry Bolla actually did come from Venice Beach, California.[4]

Like Ventura and role model "Superstar" Graham, Hulk Hogan was more of a body-builder than a wrestler. He had really wanted to be a rock musician, and was playing guitar in a small band when he was spotted by a wrestling promoter who figured he could make better use of his size and physique in the ring. More than anyone except Vince Jr. himself, Hulk Hogan ignited the firestorm of popularity that engulfed professional wrestling in the mid-1980s. TV ratings soared and wrestling programs sold out auditoriums all over the country. And there was

the merchandising, the videos, the action fig-ures, the T-shirts, the recordings. The profits were enormous.

In 1984 a feud between Hogan and Ventura was being hyped by the WWF. The pair con-fronted one another in a variety of venues throughout the country. It was all a buildup to a World Championship match that was to be held in Los Angeles. The match, and a planned world tour to follow, would have made Jesse Ventura a millionaire. But it was not to be.

The trouble started in Phoenix, when Jesse had difficulty breathing during a match. The next night he was wrestling in Oakland. He got through the match but the breathing problem was even worse. The next day he was in San Diego for the final match before his big bout with Hulk Hogan. He could barely get out of bed, and breathing was so painful that he checked himself into a hospital.

At first he thought he had pneumonia. He'd had pneumonia before and was not worried. It was much worse. He had what is called a pul-monary embolus, or to put it in layman's lan-guage, blood clots in his lungs. Doctors determined that the clot had started in his leg, broken loose, and traveled through his body to his lungs, where it had broken into smaller clots that were seriously interfering with his breathing. The real danger, however, was that the clots could travel to his heart and give him a heart attack, or to his brain and produce a stroke. He asked the doctor to give it to him straight. The doctor told Jesse Ventura that he could die at any moment.[5]

Jesse was immediately immobilized. The more he moved the greater the chance that a deadly blood clot could break loose and travel to the heart or brain. He was also put on powerful drugs to dissolve the clots. Terry flew out from Minnesota and sat by his bedside for six days, while his life literally hung in the balance.

When the immediate crisis was over, Jesse went back home to Minnesota. He was still taking powerful medication that would keep him from entering the ring for months. His chance to become a rich man wrestling Hulk Hogan all over the world was gone. And he faced the real possibility that his wrestling career—the only real job he ever had since leaving the service—was over forever.

This was a real low point in his life. Then he got a call from Vince McMahon Jr. who, as usual, had an idea. Did Jesse want to step out of the ring and get behind a microphone as a color commentator for televised matches? There had never been a commentator before who had supported the bad guys. Other commentators, including McMahon himself, always complained when they broke the rules. A guy who regularly boosted the rule breakers would be an innovation. Something the fans might enjoy. And big-mouth Jesse Ventura seemed to be made for the part.

Jesse jumped at the chance, and from Jesse "the Body" he became Jesse "the Mouth." Though he still continued to wrestle occasionally, Jesse spent more and more time as a commentator. He would announce, then wrestle, then go back behind the mike and announce again.

"You don't see Howard Cosell doin' this, do ya? I'm the only announcer in the world who can back up what he says by getting in the ring and provin' it!"

When Jesse began his announcing career for the WWF there were two teams of announcers for matches. The A team was Vince Jr. and Bruno Samartino, a former wrestling great and still one of the most popular figures in professional wrestling at the time. The B team that announced the secondary matches was former wrestler Gorilla Monsoon and Jesse. Jesse constantly derided his partner as being old and fat—he called him Gah-RIL-lah. Monsoon, really Gino Marella, weighed over 400 pounds (181 kilograms) during his ring days. He had slimmed down to something around 300 (136 kilograms) as an announcer. He took Jesse's constant jibes with a mixture of exasperation and good nature.

Samartino proved to be too colorless for the new comic-book world of WWF wrestling, and soon he was shelved. Jesse, who would show up in a pink tuxedo or some equally outlandish outfit—a different one every night—was perfect for the role. His signature line was "The pleasure is all yours." He enraged fans by calling some of their favorites, like Ricky Steamboat, "a wimp."[6] His technique for getting people to hate him, which had worked so well in the ring, worked even better behind the microphone. Jesse Ventura may not have been a first-rate wrestler. But he was a first-rate bad-guy announcer. In fact, he was actually the first bad-guy announcer. Since then every wrestling announcing team has one.

In 1987 pro wrestling hit the national TV broadcast networks when the WWF's *Saturday Night Main Event* became a summer replacement for NBC's *Saturday Night Live*. At times it even drew higher ratings than the famous comedy show. Jesse was one of the announcers on this show. It gave him national exposure and paid very well.

While most wrestling was still a cable TV staple, Vince Jr. also introduced hugely popular pay-per-view extravaganzas like "Wrestle-Mania"—loaded with nonwrestling celebrities. Here, too, Jesse was one of the announcers and he was pulling down huge fees for his work. But in wrestling, like in any other form of show business, the only certainty is uncertainty.

These photos are from Jesse's
senior class yearbook. Jesse was voted
as having the "Best Physique."

In his early years as a wrestler
Jesse played the "bad guy."

Jesse in his first movie, *The Predator*,
which starred Arnold Schwarzenegger.

Vince McMahon calling a match

Hulk Hogan,
Jesse's nemesis

Jesse is sworn in as governor of Minnesota. His wife, Terry, holds the Bible as daughter, Jade, and son, Tyrel, look on.

Jade's first major horse show was attended by Tipper Gore, center, wife of then vice president Al Gore, and Jade's mom, Terry.

Wrestler Chyna shows Governor Ventura that the sunglasses and feather boa of Jesse "the Body" Ventura can also be worn with a business suit.

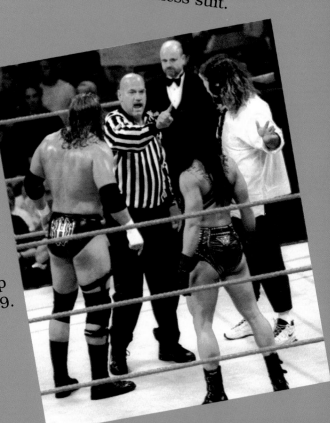

Governor Ventura takes time out for a turn back in the ring—this time as a referee at the World Wrestling Federation's Triple Threat Championship Match in August 1999.

Jesse Ventura

Governor Jesse Ventura in his office

Chapter Seven

The Actor — Despite his loudmouthed aggressiveness and macho bluster, most people who know him say that Jesse Ventura is basically a friendly guy. He may growl a lot, but he really likes people. His old wrestling trainer Jack Sharkey says that there were only two people that Jesse Ventura actually hated, AWA promoter Verne Gagne and Hulk Hogan. His reasons for hating Gagne are obvious. His reasons for hating Hogan are less obvious and more revealing.

Of course, while they were both wrestling for the WWF Ventura and Hogan had a well-publicized "feud." But like all wrestling feuds this one was manufactured, part of an elaborately scripted scenario. Behind the microphone, bad-guy announcer Ventura constantly derided and insulted Hogan, who was at that time playing the part of the good guy. That too, was all part of the script.

During the rise in popularity of WWF wrestling in the mid-1980s a lot of wrestlers resented Hogan. These feelings were not part of any script or scenario—they were very real. At this time Hulk Hogan absolutely dominated the wrestling scene. He completely eclipsed everyone else. In this world of big muscles and big egos, that was bound to generate resentment. And Hogan was making more money than anyone else—much, much more. No matter how popular a wrestler was, no matter how skilled or colorful he may have been, no matter how many risks he took and how many matches he had, he wasn't going to make anywhere near the kind of money that Hulk Hogan did. That too was bitterly resented.

The fact that Hogan's enormous popularity rubbed off on wrestling in general and helped to create an atmosphere in which everyone was making more money was not really taken into account. For wrestling, Hulk Hogan was the rising tide that lifted all boats, but Hogan's boat was a yacht and it was lifted far above the others. Years later, the popular veteran Rowdy Roddy Piper acknowledged as much in what amounted to an apology to Hulk Hogan. Jesse Ventura, on the other hand, has never apolo-

gized to his onetime friend, and insists that he has other and better reasons for harboring bitter feelings toward Hogan.

Jesse, the son of a laborer, had always chaffed at the treatment that wrestlers received from the promoters—who were in effect their bosses. He had once thought about the idea of organizing a union for wrestlers and even discussed the idea with other wrestlers, including Hulk Hogan. Hogan said it sounded like a pretty good idea. After all, most professional athletes and professional actors belong to very powerful unions. However, nothing ever came of the union idea. Later Jesse found out that Hogan had told Vince McMahon Jr. about Jesse's idea—and that made Vince Jr. very angry at Jesse.

Jesse found out what Hogan had done in testimony that Vince Jr. gave in a lawsuit Jesse filed against him. Here is how that came about. In 1991, after Jesse's connection with the WWF was severed—whether he quit or was dumped depends on whom you talk to—Jesse began wondering about all those WWF products (T-shirts, action figures, videos, etc.) featuring wrestlers, for which the wrestlers received no royalties. All profits went directly to Vince McMahon Jr. Vince Jr. was making a fortune; the wrestlers were getting nothing—except for Hulk Hogan. The superstar was getting a hefty percentage of the profits on the merchandise that featured him. But no one knew that until it was revealed in Jesse's lawsuit. That also angered Jesse and turned him fully against his former friend.

Well before the final break with the WWF, Jesse was getting restless with his wrestling announcer role. Along the way he had picked up an agent, Barry Bloom, who helped guide his career into other areas. One of the first areas was to get Jesse a job as a color commentator for the Tampa Bay Buccaneers football team.

Jesse had played some football in high school and college, though he was never particularly adept at the sport. He had no previous interest in the Florida team; he was a Minnesota Vikings fan. But in 1989 the Buccaneers were a horrible team. Not only did they have an abysmal record, they had a hard time getting more than 15,000 fans into the stadium for home games. Ratings for broadcasts of Bucs games were in the cellar. So the radio station that broadcast the Bucs tried to generate a little excitement by hiring a colorful, charismatic outsider, Jesse Ventura.

Bucs management was horrified at first that the radio station was planning to hire a wrestler. That, they insisted, would make a mockery of the team. Station management retorted that it was hard to make any more of a mockery of the Bucs than they already were.[1]

In the end the collaboration worked out pretty well for Jesse and the team. Jesse attracted a lot of attention to the Bucs and at times seemed to be a bigger attraction than the

team itself. Jesse worked in the broadcast booth with two more-experienced football announcers. He toned down his bellicose wrestling announcer persona, rooted loyally for the Florida team, and generally behaved like a complete professional.

But after two seasons a different station bought the rights to broadcast the Bucs, and they wanted a new image. So Jesse was let go. He really didn't care because he was now much more interested in becoming a movie actor.

Bloom got Jesse a shot at a part in a new Arnold Schwarzenegger film, *Predator*. To hear Jesse tell the story, the casting director Jackie Burch "couldn't take her eyes off me."[2] Probably not. There he stood, a huge hulking man whose presence filled the room. His hair was shoulder length and bleached blond, and his mustache was a menacing Fu Manchu style. He wore half a dozen earrings and had a voice that sounded like gravel being poured into a bucket, loudly.

He was hired almost at once.

The film is an action flick with lots of gunfire, muscle flexing, and macho posturing. It's about a group of commandos who are sent to South America to kill an alien monster that has been killing and eating American soldiers. Jesse plays Blain, an over-the-top, tough-talking, gun-toting character who regards himself as the toughest guy in the bunch.

It really isn't much of a part. Blain gets killed less than halfway through the picture.

Jesse had only a few lines of dialogue, and said that he had to fight for every one of them. His most famous line, indeed his only memorable line, is "I ain't got time to bleed." Later the line was to become Jesse's unofficial slogan, and he even used it as the title for his best-selling autobiography.

The film was shot in Mexico. Jesse became good friends with the star, Arnold Schwarzenegger. The two men had a lot in common. They were both dedicated bodybuilders. There is one story Jesse repeats with relish. Schwarzenegger brought down a lot of his own gym equipment and set it up in a room. He gave Jesse the key and told him he could work out whenever he wanted to. At first Jesse and Arnold would both work out from five to six in the morning, before shooting started. If Jesse failed to work out one morning Arnold would rag him about it all day.

So Jesse started getting up earlier, and at a quarter to five he was in the gym before Arnold and his bodyguard Sven came in. He would pour water all over himself to look as if he was drenched with sweat from working out for a long time. Arnold saw this and decided he had to get up earlier because he couldn't let Jesse outtrain him. They kept getting up earlier and earlier until they were both in the gym at four in the morning.

Jesse Ventura had a great deal of admiration for Arnold Schwarzenegger. Schwarzenegger was extremely smart, highly motivated, and

very ambitious; he started as a bodybuilder and became a movie star and a millionaire many times over.[3]

Jesse enjoyed making the film, but what he loved most of all was the idea of being a movie star. On the promotional tour for the film it was first class all the way. He insisted on bringing his wife Terry along on the tour, which rather surprised the movie promotion people, but they picked up her tab without a murmur.

There were limos and hotel suites that must have cost a thousand dollars a night. One of them had a grand piano and a four-person Jacuzzi in the bedroom. The old South Side Boy from Minneapolis reveled in the luxury. He was like a kid in a candy store. "I wonder what the poor people are doing today," he thought, and then added, "Isn't that awful?"

He started the trip with $235 in his pocket. Three weeks later he still had $235. He was living in luxury and hadn't spent a penny of his own money.

Predator was Jesse's first film, and though he probably wouldn't admit it, it was really the high point of his movie career. He was in *The Running Man*, another Schwarzenegger vehicle. He was paid a lot more and even had a larger part—but the film never really took off like *Predator*. And there were no memorable lines. After that there were a number of small parts in some forgettable films, and a brief appearance in an episode of *The X-Files* on television. He had one starring role in something called

Abraxas, Guardian of the Universe, a truly awful low-budget science-fiction film. His last film was the high budget *Batman & Robin*, but he only had a bit part. If you blink you might miss him.

He made some commercials and filmed episodes for a TV series called *Tag Team* about a couple of professional wrestlers who became cops, but the series was canceled before it aired. He was also announcer of a short-lived syndicated show called *Grudge Match*, in which a couple of contenders who had a score to settle fought it out with spaghetti or oversized boxing gloves. It was pretty bad.

The offers were not pouring in as he had hoped, and soon Jesse Ventura was looking for work again. He wasn't going to find it with the WWF. Not only had Jesse skipped out on broadcasts while making films, he had actually sued Vince McMahon Jr. It was about money, of course.

Vince McMahon Jr. is not the raging, vindictive psychotic that he appears to be on TV. That is just a character he plays, as the various wrestlers play different characters in the ongoing soap opera that is professional wrestling.[4] But Vince Jr. has been top dog in professional wrestling for many years. It is a very tough and competitive business. In order to stay on top you have to be a very tough businessman, and Vince Jr. is certainly that. He hates to be crossed in his own realm, and he wins most of the fights he gets involved with. Wrestling may

be fake, but the wrestling business certainly isn't.

Ultimately Jesse won his case and collected over $800,000. He regularly boasted that he was the guy who had sued Vince McMahon Jr. and won! Vince Jr. wasn't going to forget that and give Jesse Ventura a job anytime soon.

But there was a new player in the wrestling business, media mogul Ted Turner. Turner was trying to develop his own wrestling federation, World Championship Wrestling (WCW), to provide wrestling programs for his cable network and to compete with McMahon's WWF, which had come to completely dominate the lucrative business of televised wrestling.

Turner had deep pockets, and he began hiring big names to attract wrestling fans. One of those he hired was Jesse Ventura, for a sizable salary. By this time Jesse wasn't doing any wrestling at all—he was strictly an announcer. But he was a marquee name. Wrestling fans knew who he was. And he was probably worth the money he was paid. Slowly the WCW began to establish itself as a respectable and profitable competitor to WWF.

But Jesse was losing interest in being a wrestling announcer. He didn't keep up with the ever-changing wrestling world as he once had. His performance fell off, he got fewer chances to announce, and ultimately he and the WCW parted ways.

He served briefly as a color commentator for the Minnesota Vikings football team. At least it was a team he knew and liked. But that didn't work out either. He only lasted one season. The career of Jesse "the Body" Ventura seemed to be going downhill, but in fact, it was just about to make a series of rather remarkable turns.

Chapter Eight

The Mayor

To Jesse Ventura his entry into politics was "destiny."

Jesse always had a lively interest in politics and current events—lively, that is, for a professional wrestler. However, he often neglected to vote. And while he had an opinion about practically everything, he didn't always have the information to back it up.

In 1983, Jesse and his family moved to the city of Brooklyn Park, Minnesota, on the west bank of the Mississippi and about 10 miles (16 kilometers) northwest of the Minneapolis–St. Paul area. It is really more of a suburb than a city. The college Jesse once attended was located there. It's a pleasant place with lots of parks and other green areas, and had a population of about 56,000 in 1990. It was close enough to a major metropolitan area to be convenient, but spread out enough to give residents at least a feel of the country. But this popular area was growing rapidly, and with growth came inevitable problems and conflicts.

The mayor of the town—an unpaid part-time position—was Jim Krautkremer, who managed computer operations for a large Minneapolis company. He was first elected mayor in 1972, when the old mayor decided not to run for reelection, and he just kept on getting reelected without much, if any, opposition. He served on all sorts of regional boards and associations and generally thought that he was doing a good job for the city.

Then in 1987 a local developer announced that he was going to build some houses on a wetland area of Brooklyn Park's West River Road. Those who lived in the area didn't like that idea at all and they organized to put pressure on the city in a variety of ways to stop the development. The city council, led by Mayor Krautkremer, voted seven to nothing to allow the development, and that really angered area residents.

It is the sort of dispute that arises regularly in every growing area. The difference here was that one of the West River Road area residents who didn't like the idea of a new development was Jesse "the Body" Ventura.

The first time Mayor Krautkremer even became aware of Jesse's existence was at a city council meeting when some big guy with red and green hair kept jumping up and interrupting him in a loud, gravelly voice. The mayor kept gaveling him down.

One of the councilmen leaned over to the mayor and said, "Do you know who that was?"

The mayor said he didn't.

"That was Jesse Ventura."

The mayor, no wrestling fan, had never heard the name before. Shortly he was to hear almost nothing else.[1]

Some of Jesse's neighbors and allies in the fight against development began urging him to run for mayor in the next election, which was to be held in 1990. Jesse didn't think seriously about the idea at first, because he was pretty busy.

But in 1990 several things happened, or to be more accurate, several things stopped happening. That was the year he had his final blowup with Vince Jr. and was summarily fired from his announcing position at the WWF. He had planned to go out to Los Angeles to start shooting the TV series *Tag Team*. But the series was canceled. Quite suddenly and unexpectedly Jesse had some time on his hands—enough time to run for mayor. That is what he calls "destiny."

At a meeting where Jesse said that he might run for mayor one of the mayor's friends shouted, "You can't win." That made Jesse even madder and more determined than ever.

Jesse has denounced Brooklyn Park's old administration as "one of the greediest packs of good old boys in the state." He said that they were in the developers' "back pockets," that they had built a lavish clubhouse near the public golf course with the taxpayer's money. He made the part-time mayor of this suburban area sound like the boss of a big-city machine. A lot of the charges he made were, in typical Ventura fashion, outrageous and over the top.

But one charge, and the one that really made up the core of Jesse Ventura's campaign, was that the mayor and his supporters on the city council had lost touch with the voters of Brooklyn Park. And that charge was absolutely on target.

Politics in Brooklyn Park were not very exciting. In 1987, during the election before Jesse ran, only 2,632 voters even bothered to show up to vote. City council meetings were poorly attended. Most people had little or no idea what the city government was doing. They may have grumbled privately about this or that, but no one had ever organized or focused their dissatisfaction, until Jesse came along.

Even Jesse's opponents had to admit that he ran a terrific campaign. "We launched a very grassroots, plainspoken kind of campaign," he said. "I don't think we spent more than two or three thousand dollars."

His volunteers, mostly local people recruited from the antidevelopment fight, knocked on doors, distributed leaflets, put up signs, and stuffed envelopes. Jesse himself seemed to be everywhere. He wasn't a traditional candidate and didn't look like one. He wore Zubaz—a brightly colored, baggy brand of pants made by a Minnesota company—a baseball cap, and a T-shirt. Casual was hardly the word for the way he dressed. He was always giving interviews, some of them to national publications like *USA Today*, who were intrigued by this strange phenomenon. He said he would have city council meetings televised—"I love performing for the camera."

When election day rolled around the voters turned out in record numbers. Some of the increase in voter turnout was due to some high-profile statewide races that were on the ballot. But a lot of it was due to Jesse.

When the votes were counted Jesse had won in a landslide, 12,778 votes to 7,390. He carried every one of the city's twenty-one precincts.[2] While the victory had been expected, Jesse still seemed a bit stunned by it. And he was irritated when a reporter asked him if he was going to appoint the wrestler Nature Boy Ric Flair head of the streets department. He insisted that the election was no joke; he was serious and he wanted to do a good job for his community.

Jesse's election as mayor of Brooklyn Park was one part of his emerging political career.

Talk radio was the other part. Talk radio was a phenomenon that exploded in the 1990s. As the decade began there were about three hundred talk/news radio stations in the entire country. A few years later there were over one thousand.

Talk radio is difficult to characterize—it is somewhere between entertainment, political commentary, and screaming abuse. Some hosts like Rush Limbaugh and G. Gordon Liddy had definite political agendas that they pushed relentlessly for hours every day. Others like Howard Stern and Don Imus regarded themselves more as entertainers. But even they could be extremely influential. They had large and devoted followings and their opinions on any subject, including politics, could be extremely influential, and they knew it.

In addition to the national stars whose syndicated shows could be heard practically everywhere in the country, there were hundreds and hundreds of local talk radio hosts, many of them quite popular and influential in their own areas. For several hours each day these hosts would field phone calls from listeners, interview guests, and deliver their own opinions on a large variety of subjects.

While there was a good deal of difference between hosts, most shared certain characteristics. The vast majority were male, and they appealed to a male audience. Politically they tended to be conservative or "populist"—that is,

they claimed to represent the "common man" or "ordinary guy" as opposed to "the government" or some vague but powerful group known as "the establishment." They were not afraid to talk frankly and loudly about anything, including things they knew nothing about. They could be outrageous—indeed that was a large part of their appeal. And they were usually rude and overbearing to people who disagreed with them.

Is this beginning to sound like someone you have heard of? Jesse Ventura was a natural for the talk radio of the 1990s. But he sort of fell into it in an odd way. Destiny again?

In 1991 young Tyrel Ventura called a local radio station. The producer knew whose son Tyrel was, and they began to regularly use a segment about Ty "the Boy" Ventura. The following year that same producer was working at a talk radio station in a St. Paul suburb. He remembered Ty "the Boy" and thought that Jesse "the Body" or more probably Jesse "the Mouth," might make a good radio talk-show host. So he called him up and left a message on his answering machine. The mayor of Brooklyn Park called back as soon as he received the message. Aside from his duties as mayor, which were neither time consuming nor profitable, Jesse didn't have much to do.

A deal was worked out and in January 1993, *The Jesse Ventura Show* began running on KSTP-AM from 5:30 to 9:00 every weekday morning. Jesse never really adjusted to the early morning hours, but after a few months he adjusted to the other demands of talk radio very well. It was a job he loved.

Jesse thought things at KSTP were going along great. Early in 1996 he had signed a new two-year contract. Then one day during the summer he was told that the morning show would be taken "in a new direction," and that he wouldn't have to come to work the next day. He was being fired.

The reasons for his sudden dismissal are a matter of dispute. KSTP management said his ratings were dropping, but they admit that they handled the dismissal badly. Jesse insists that his ratings were just fine and he was dismissed because he had become too controversial. Whatever the reason, Jesse Ventura was out of work, and he was very angry.

By this time Jesse was well known and he had a following, so he immediately got another offer from rival station KFAN, primarily a sports talk station. But he was still under contract to KSTP and legally blocked from taking another broadcasting job. It was nearly a year before he got back on the radio again. He told KFAN that he didn't want to do a morning show—getting up at 3:30 A.M. was just too hard. So they gave him the mid-afternoon slot and he was an immediate hit. He talked sports, but he talked about a lot of other things, including politics.

And he settled a few personal scores as well. When Hulk Hogan came to Minneapolis for

some matches Jesse attacked him brutally for days. Later Hogan told friends he wasn't going to wrestle in Minnesota anymore.

On the political front, Jesse's term as mayor of Brooklyn Park was surprisingly unspectacular and uneventful. In reality the unpaid part-time mayor of the town didn't have the power to do anything very spectacular. In addition, while Jesse was the mayor the city council was still made up primarily of his opponents, and his power was even more limited.

He was accused of being a publicity hound, of being arrogant and brutally rude to his political opponents at council meetings, being inattentive to his job, and missing too many meetings because of his other interests. But the city ran smoothly during his term, and it is undeniable that Jesse Ventura's presence rekindled interest in local politics. Despite his wildman image, he did not try to run the city like a wildman, and the charges that were leveled against him are the sort that are routinely leveled at mayors all over the country by their opponents.

In 1994, Jesse announced that he was not going to run for reelection. That was a decision he had to make because he was preparing to move out of Brooklyn Park altogether, and by law the mayor had to live in the city. The Ventura family bought a two-acre ranch outside the city. It was a place where Terry could raise and train horses—riding had been a passion all her life. There was also plenty of room for Ty and Jade and for Bernice Janos. Jesse's mother had lived with them since the death of her husband in 1991, and her health was failing.

His term as mayor, plus his talk radio show, had whetted Jesse's appetite for politics. And Jesse Ventura's astonishing life was going to take the most astonishing turn yet.

Chapter Nine

The Candidate

Jesse Ventura insists, "The idea of running for governor really sneaked up on me." The "sneaking" was by Dean Barkley, one of those politically obsessed people who is always running for some political office or the other and always losing—indeed, barely being noticed.

In 1994, Barkley was running for the U.S. Senate as the candidate of something called the Independence party. His major campaign issue was that he wasn't either a Democrat or a Republican. As usual he was barely noticed by the media—except for talk show host Jesse Ventura. Jesse liked Dean Barkley and had him as a guest repeatedly. He even agreed to become honorary chairman of Barkley's next campaign in 1996. Dean Barkley was just the sort of independent, antiestablishment, plain-talking guy who appealed to Jesse. But he was a colorless campaigner.

When the two appeared together, Jesse got all the cheers. Barkley, as usual, was barely noticed. Finally he told Jesse that the wrong guy was running, and it was Jesse who should be running for higher office. Jesse responded that he didn't want to run for senator because he didn't want to go to Washington. But he might run for governor, because if he won he could stay in Minnesota. He was half joking, but only half. And the compulsive candidate Dean Barkley was not about to let him get away.[1]

By 1996 the Minnesota Independence party had become part of the Reform party. The Reform party was the creation of Texas billion-aire Ross Perot. Perot was a funny-looking little jug-eared guy with a high nasal twang and a quick wit. He had a lot of money to spend on his own campaign for president, but it wasn't just his money that made him so popular. He didn't have a specific program; in fact, it was hard to figure out where he stood on most issues.

His main campaign theme was that he was not one of the other guys. He was an independent who talked straight and used common sense. If there was a problem he would "roll up his sleeves, look under the hood, and fix it." He would be guided by the will of the people. "I'm

Ross. You're the Boss," he would tell voters. And people listened. He got into the presidential debates, where many felt he outshone both President George Bush and his Democratic challenger Governor Bill Clinton. Ross Perot didn't win the election, but he did get nearly 20 percent of the vote nationwide, and a higher percentage in Minnesota. It was an astounding performance for a third-party candidate.

Minnesota is a highly political state, and has produced an exceptionally large number of extremely prominent and sometimes offbeat political figures. In 1938, Harold Stassen was elected as the youngest governor in state history. He served until 1943. After that he ran for the Republican nomination for president ten times and lost every time, setting a record that will probably never be broken.

In 1968, Minnesota senator Eugene McCarthy challenged Vice President Hubert H. Humphrey, also from Minnesota, for the Democratic presidential nomination. And later another Minnesota senator, Walter Mondale, became vice president and an unsuccessful Democratic candidate for president. The electorate is unpredictable. One of Minnesota's current senators is among the most liberal in Congress; the other, among the most conservative. It is a state in which, politically speaking, almost anything can happen. Even so, Jesse Ventura came as a surprise.

Jesse was being pressed by the leaders of the Minnesota Reform party to run for governor. Despite Perot's good showing in the state, the Reform party had never actually succeeded in getting anyone elected to anything, anywhere. With a character as colorful as Jesse Ventura at the head of the ticket, the party could at least be assured that it would not be ignored.

Jesse liked the idea. Terry was nowhere near as enthusiastic; in fact, she was against it. Finally she agreed, though Jesse admits that she probably wasn't convinced. He just wore her down. "I'm not an easy guy to say no to."

In January 1988, Jesse Ventura stood in front of a group of reporters on the steps of the Minnesota State Capitol and announced that he was running for governor on the Reform party ticket. He stood alone. He didn't want to use his family as a background for a photo opportunity. Though normally very friendly and outgoing, Terry did not like the idea of campaigning as "the candidate's wife." She stayed home with the kids and the horses.

As expected, the press took notice of Jesse's announcement. But they didn't take it very seriously. They seemed to think it was some sort of publicity stunt, perhaps to draw attention to his radio show.

Jesse had the Reform party nomination sewed up; there was no real opposition. But in the general election he would face some political heavyweights. There was to be a primary in the Democratic party. One of the candidates was Hubert "Skip" Humphrey, the state's attor-

ney general and son of the late senator and vice president. Another was Ted Mondale, also the son of a former senator and vice president. There was also a former governor's son, a millionaire, and a few others. Humphrey eventually won the primary. The Republican side was less complicated. The heavy favorite was Norm Coleman, the mayor of St. Paul. In this company Jesse was the ultimate outsider. He was also being outspent by everyone. When the campaign began Jesse had $244 in actual campaign funds.

But as the campaign began, Jesse began to surprise people. His name was already well known in the state. But most Minnesotans expected this huge, shaven-headed man, who had been a professional wrestler and talk radio screamer, to come on as some sort of howling Neanderthal. Instead, Jesse "the Candidate" could be charming, funny, and most of all real. He didn't sound like a candidate; he sounded like an ordinary but decent guy who understood the lives and aspirations of ordinary people. Sometimes his frankness got him into trouble, but it was a lot better than if he had sounded evasive, shifty, or given "canned" answers.

Education was a big issue. Jesse stressed that he had gone to Minnesota public schools, his kids were in Minnesota public schools, and for good measure he chose Mae Schunk, a sixty-four-year-old former schoolteacher, as his running mate for lieutenant governor. No long public policy statement was going to do more to convince voters of his commitment to education.[2]

A series of public debates between the candidates was scheduled. Democrat Humphrey insisted that Jesse be included because he thought Jesse, a conservative on matters of spending and government programs, would draw more votes away from his Republican contender Coleman. Coleman agreed because he felt that Jesse, a social liberal, would take votes away from Democrat Humphrey.

In the first televised debate between the three candidates the question of gay rights was raised. The state legislature had passed a "Defense of Marriage Act," banning the state from recognizing gay or lesbian marriages that might have been performed in other states. The Republican and Democratic candidates gave moralistic or legalistic answers. Jesse's answer was surprising, simple, and touching. "I have two friends who have been together for forty-one years. If one of them becomes sick, the other one is not even allowed to be at his bedside. I don't believe the government should be so hostile, so mean spirited. . . . Love is bigger than government."[3]

With answers like that, Jesse won the first televised debate hands down. He never had a prepared statement, and never used notes. He spoke, he said, "from the heart." And the two major candidates were beginning to wonder if letting Jesse into the debates had been such a great idea after all.

Jesse's campaign began attracting media attention, not only in Minnesota but nationally. His numbers were rising in the polls and he was able to get enough money to do some media advertising. In radio ads where he discussed issues Jesse wound up by saying, "I believe that Led Zeppelin and the Rolling Stones are two of the best rock bands of all times." Major party candidates just couldn't say things like that.

One of Jesse's TV spots became an instant legend in the world of political advertising. It was based on the famous statue by Rodin called "The Thinker," in which a nude muscular man sits with his chin resting on his hand, looking as if he is, well, thinking. The ad shows what appears to be a nearly nude Jesse sitting in The Thinker's pose. Actually, a body double was used, because forty-seven-year-old Jesse had been putting on weight and no longer possessed the sculptured physique of his wrestling days. But Jesse was used for the close-ups.

The ad said how the THE BODY was now THE MIND, and explained all the good things he was going to do for the state. At the very end the camera panned in on Jesse's face—he smiled slightly and winked. It was absolutely charming. It showed voters that Jesse Ventura wasn't one of those solemn politicians people had come to dislike and distrust—he had a sense of humor, even about himself.

Jesse was also an enormously energetic campaigner. Just before the election Jesse went on a seventy-two-hour, thirty-four-stop campaign swing throughout the state. He insists that during that period he didn't get any sleep at all, but that was less than half of what he had experienced during SEALs Hell Week. The campaign rented a couple of RV's and with an ever-increasing caravan of media people in pursuit, they barnstormed the state. He was popular wherever he went, and he was getting the kind of media attention that no amount of money could buy. His momentum was building, and even Terry joined the caravan. It was the first campaigning she had done.

Though Jesse now says that he had been confident that he would win for a long time, there is considerable evidence to show that up until the last few days he figured he had given the professionals a good run and had a lot of fun. But he didn't think he was going to become governor. Last-minute polls showed that the three candidates were in a virtual statistical dead heat. And Jesse was winning big among young voters eighteen to twenty-four. He was also popular among people who didn't usually bother to vote—people who were angry at all politicians and figured it didn't make any difference who won, so why bother.

For Jesse everything depended on the turnout. Would those young voters who often didn't vote go to the polls? Would the angry and disaffected voters now feel that they had something to vote for? The voters did turn out in record numbers. Across the nation that elec-

tion day the average voter turnout was 37 percent. In Minnesota, it was 61 percent—the highest voter turnout in the nation.

The Democrats were bringing busloads of college students, first-time voters, to the polls, only to discover that their buses were filled with Ventura voters. The Republicans assumed, correctly, that Jesse would draw more votes from the Democratic candidate. But they never believed that he would get enough votes to overwhelm them as well.

That night Jesse was as surprised as anyone. Even after the TV networks declared him the winner he remained cautious. All the votes hadn't been counted yet. But the state police were already on the scene ready to escort and protect the new governor-elect. A short time later Democrat Humphrey and Republican Coleman called to concede. Finally Jesse was convinced. The final returns were Humphrey, 28 percent, Coleman 35 percent, and Ventura 37 percent. He didn't get a majority of the votes, but in a three-way race, it was a solid win.

Janos the Dirty, Jesse the Body, Jesse the Mouth, Jesse the Mind had been elected governor. Terry was overwhelmed. She broke down in tears. She was going to be first lady of the state. "I don't know how to do this. I don't know what they expect me to be."[4]

"Just be yourself," her mother told her. That calmed her down and she took Jesse's hand as they went out to greet cheering supporters, eager reporters, the citizens of Minnesota, and indeed the citizens of America in general. There were a lot of other elections being decided that night. But the really big story was the election of Jesse Ventura.[5]

Maria Shriver of NBC, who also happens to be Arnold Schwarzenegger's wife, was able to snag the first national TV interview with the newly elected governor. Suddenly everybody wanted to talk to him.

The celebration went on long into the night. Jesse says with his alarming yet disarming frankness, "I was destined to greet my first full day as governor-elect with a hangover."

Chapter Ten

The Future

Shortly after he was elected governor, Jesse Ventura paid a visit to the Minnesota State Capitol building. It's one of those big official buildings with brass-bound doors, marble staircases, and columns. He was looking for the governor's office that was soon to be his office. And he didn't even know where it was.

In his wanderings he passed a display of larger-than-life painted portraits of former Minnesota governors. And he knew that one day his portrait would be up there too, "in wraparound shades, tights, and a feather boa," he thought.[1]

Jesse was as irreverent as ever, but a bit awed by the responsibility that had suddenly been thrust upon him. He wasn't wearing his feather boa that day. He wasn't even wearing his more familiar T-shirt and jeans. He started wearing business suits with conservative ties. But the problem was that Jesse Ventura stuffed into a suit that would never fit him properly looked even bigger and more forbidding than Jesse Ventura in T-shirt and jeans.

Aside from his time in the navy, Jesse Ventura had always lived pretty much by his own rules. He did what he wanted. He said what he wanted. And if other people didn't like it that was their problem. Now he was surrounded by state police. He was on call twenty-four hours a day. His every move, his every utterance, was carefully watched and recorded. "I felt a little bit like a prisoner. I've never had this many restrictions in my life," he complained.

Inauguration Day, January 4, 1999, was a typical Minnesota winter day. There had been a blizzard. The roads were covered with snow and ice, and many were impassable. The temperature was eleven below zero with a windchill factor that made it feel much worse.

That didn't bother one of Jesse's inaugural guests, Arnold Schwarzenegger. "For a real man the cold weather means nothing," he bragged to a reporter.[2]

Jesse, looking uncomfortable in his black suit, took the oath of office and gave his inaugural speech. As usual it was not a prepared speech, and he had no notes. He began by recounting how a group of high school students

told him that he should not use a prepared speech. "'We want to hear from your heart and we want to hear from your soul.' So that's what you're going to get. I'm not changing."

At one point he admitted that he had to read something. He pulled out a pair of glasses, "And yes, when you get to be forty-seven, these become part of your uniform," and read a congratulatory note from one of his previous SEAL instructors, who happened to be on the platform with him.

"I'm sure you must be nervous and apprehensive, maybe even a little frightened about that challenge ahead of you. But keep this in mind, you've been there. You've been pushed, tried and tested by the best, and you've passed with flying colors . . ."

Jesse's inaugural speech was amazingly short—it took about five minutes. He ended by raising his right hand in the air, making a fist, and giving the old SEAL cheer:

"HOOYAH!"

The inaugural ball was even less conventional. Jesse wore a shirt and vest so blindingly colorful that they recalled his old wrestling days. He even had what looked like a feather boa draped around his neck. He had sunglasses and three earrings. A bright bandanna covered his shaved head. He told 13,000 screaming supporters: "LET'S PARTY!"[3]

And party they did. At one point rocker Warren Zevon invited Jesse to sing along with him. During his career Jesse briefly had his own rock band. He rather ruefully admitted that he probably enjoyed his performances more than his audience did. But this night everyone in the audience enjoyed hearing the governor-elect rock.

The big question now was could Jesse Ventura govern? He had won the three-way election with only 37 percent of the vote. There was not a single member of the Reform party in the legislature. If he was to get anything done he would have to do it by working with Republicans and Democrats, members of the traditional parties he scorned.

And there was even a bigger question. Would Jesse self-destruct? Remember, Jesse always said he had a talent for irritating people. He often called himself a "Klingon"—a reference to the surly warrior race in the *Star Trek* TV series. Could a self-described Klingon be governor of a midwestern state? Would this inexperienced, aggressive, confrontational, outspoken, and wildly unconventional man do things and say things that would enrage so many people that he would be driven out of office? His opponents predicted that he would.

One of his fiercest opponents turned out to be Garrison Keillor, a normally gentle Minnesota humorist who is well known nationally for his syndicated radio show, *Prairie Home Companion*. Keillor was outraged and deeply offended by Jesse: "The Governor, in plain English, is a Yahoo who has never confessed to a single regret or second thought and who struts around St. Paul, a big small town, with a retinue of bodyguards, emitting a great air of celebrity. . . . eventually you have to tell him to shut the hell up. He isn't a danger to anybody . . . He's just big, loud and arrogant . . . and all we needed was someone to run the government."

Jesse responded by saying that he never listened to Keillor's radio show, but noted that it appeared on National Public Radio, which received government funds, and he didn't like the idea of taxpayer money going for anything like that. Despite his macho bluster, Jesse has a pretty thin skin about criticism.

Jesse also became the target of cartoonist Gary Trudeau in his popular *Doonesbury* strip. What many critics overlooked is that while Jesse's *style* was unconventional, his politics were quite mainstream. The conservative side preached lower taxes, more self-reliance, and strongly opposed gun control and government control in general. On the liberal side, he was for a woman's right to chose an abortion, gay rights, strong on environmental issues, and a fanatic on campaign finance reform. He was also very strong on educational issues—which had an appeal across the board.

When it came to choosing his cabinet and other advisers, Jesse Ventura went right down the middle picking from both Republicans and Democrats, a safe, stable centrist group. Then he did something completely and endearingly off the wall—he declared February 15 to be Rolling Stones day in Minnesota. That was popular with lots of people.

Under the decidedly unradical Ventura administration the state of Minnesota rolled on very well. In many respects Jesse and the state were lucky. The previous administration had left the state in good financial condition. Indeed, good times throughout the United States at the end of the millennium left most states in good financial condition. It's much easier for a governor to be popular when his or her state isn't facing a huge budget gap. Governors throughout the United States were generally more popular than they had been in a long time. Even some of Jesse's bitterest enemies had to admit they were surprised at how well he was doing. They had believed that the former wrestler would not be able to govern at all.

In the months that followed his surprise election, Jesse became one of the most sought after celebrities in the country. He was even sought by his old adversary, Vince McMahon Jr. of the WWF. Never one to hold a grudge when money and publicity are involved, Vince Jr. asked Jesse—the man who had sued him and won—to be a guest referee at the 1999 edition of his pay-per-view extravaganza "Wrestle-Mania." Jesse agreed but insisted that his huge fee go to charity. The spectacle, and particularly Jesse's performance, shocked and outraged Garrison Keillor, who may never have witnessed a wrestling performance before.

Another advantage of being a celebrity was that it gave Jesse a chance to do a guest shot on his favorite soap opera, *The Young and the*

Restless. The director declared that Jesse was "a natural," and if he ever got tired of politics he could get a job acting in the soaps.

Jesse Ventura loved the limelight, and while he didn't get along well with much of the Minnesota media, he was the darling of the national media—and he freely gave interviews to practically anyone who asked. His habit of saying whatever came to his mind, often without considering what effect it might have, could get him in trouble. He wasn't a wrestling announcer or a talk/radio show host anymore. He was governor of a large state, and people paid more attention to what he said. In a typically free-wheeling interview that he gave to *Playboy* magazine in the spring of 1999, Jesse got himself into trouble with some slighting remarks that he made about organized religion—"a sham and a crutch for weak-minded people who need strength in numbers."

That remark even shook people who tolerantly excused many of Jesse's other outrageous and provocative statements as being "just Jesse." His phenomenally high approval ratings plummeted. And Jesse, whose informal motto has always been "never apologize," admitted to second thoughts and suggested that in the future he might be a little more careful about what he said and how he said it. He also said that he was going to spend more of his time and effort simply governing the state of Minnesota and that is what he really wanted to talk about.

His popularity began to rebound.

Almost from the moment of his election the question was asked whether Jesse Ventura would run for president. At first the question wasn't a serious one. Shortly after Jesse's election Hulk Hogan began hinting very publicly that he might run for president. After all, he noted that he had been a bigger wrestling star than Jesse and could win a bigger office. Jesse dismissed Hogan's statements as "hype," and that is exactly what they turned out to be.

Jesse was not quite as dismissive of the possibility that he might run for president or some other office. But he insisted that he had made a commitment to the people of Minnesota and would serve out his entire four-year term as governor. After that—well, who could predict.

However, in 1999, speculation about a Jesse Ventura run for the presidency was not entirely unreasonable. He was the highest elected official of the Reform party and the party's most famous member, overshadowing even party founder Ross Perot. The national Reform party had some 12 million dollars of federal election funds in its treasury to mount a presidential campaign in the 2000 election. That was nowhere near what the Republican and Democratic parties would have for the election—but it would be enough for any candidate to conduct a respectable national campaign.

Perot himself indicated that he wasn't going to run again. The party had no platform, no consistent ideology, and no real organization;

and it didn't have an active leader anymore. The struggle for control of the party and its election funds was fierce and sometimes bizarre, with people like flamboyant millionaire Donald Trump and actor Warren Beatty being mentioned as possible presidential candidates.

The real campaign to take over the Reform party and its money was mounted by Pat Buchanan, a far-right ideologue who quit the Republican party because it wasn't conservative enough for him. Buchanan was politically sophisticated and media savvy. Except on an issue like gun control—which they both opposed—Ventura and Buchanan agreed on practically nothing.

When it looked as if Buchanan and his well-organized supporters were on the verge of taking over the Reform party (which they ultimately did), Jesse simply quit the party. His ties had never been that strong anyway, and there was no way that he was ever going to support Pat Buchanan for anything. Without the possibility of the Reform party and its treasury backing a Jesse Ventura for president movement, the talk of Jesse running in 2000 died away.

But Jesse Ventura has not disappeared, and is not likely to. He has become a popular figure for independent voters throughout the country; particularly for independent voters who are young or feel alienated by the current two party system. Jesse talks their language.

During the 2000 presidential campaign he was courted by both Democratic nominee Al

Gore and Green party candidate Ralph Nader. He still remains the most lively and quotable political figure in the country. Even Ventura basher Garrison Keillor admits: "He speaks plain English with none of the circuitous posturing and preening of public officials . . ."

Unless he self-destructs in some spectacular way—always a possibility for someone like Jesse—the chances are that he is going to be a force in American politics for some time to come. Not so much in his politics—they are quite unremarkable—but in his style. Don't expect to see many candidates with feather boas, but a looser dress code and at least the appearance of straight and candid talk will become more popular on the campaign trail because of Jesse's influence. He has been able to reach a huge class of voters and potential voters who otherwise had no interest in politics. You may be one of them.

Jesse Ventura probably is not going to be elected president. He may not even run for president. Not that he doubts he could win, but he says there is too much stress in the job. Presidents, Jesse notes, go into office looking young and virile. Four years later they look as if they had aged twenty years. Besides, his wife would never stand for it. "I wouldn't put any money on there ever being a Jesse 'the Prez' Ventura."

On the other hand, would you have been willing to bet on Jesse "the Gov" Ventura? I sure wouldn't have.

Notes

Chapter 1

1. Jesse Ventura, *I Ain't Got Time to Bleed* (New York: Villard, 1999), p. 42.
2. Ventura, p. 44.
3. Jake Tapper, *Body Slam* (New York: St. Martin's, 1999), p. 11.
4. Ventura, p. 45.

Chapter 2

1. Jake Tapper, *Body Slam* (New York: St. Martin's, 1999), p. 16.
2. Jesse Ventura, *I Ain't Got Time to Bleed* (New York: Villard, 1999), p. 62.
3. Tapper, p. 25.
4. Ventura, p. 75.
5. Tapper, pp. 33–34.

Chapter 3

1. Jesse Ventura, *I Ain't Got Time to Bleed* (New York: Villard, 1999), p. 86.
2. Jake Tapper, *Body Slam* (New York: St. Martin's, 1999), pp. 38–39.
3. Tapper, p. 39.

Chapter 4

1. Dan Cohen, *Wrestling Renegades* (New York: Pocket Books, 1999), p. 14.
2. Jesse Ventura, *I Ain't Got Time to Bleed* (New York: Villard, 1999), p. 90.
3. Captain Lou Albano, Bert Randolph Sugar, and Roger Woodson, *The Complete Idiot's Guide to Pro Wrestling* (New York: Alpha Books, 1999), pp 28–29.
4. Albano, p. 29.
5. Ventura, p. 91.

Chapter 5

1. Captain Lou Albano, Bert Randolph Sugar, and Roger Woodson, *The Complete Idiot's Guide to Pro Wrestling* (New York: Alpha Books, 1999). pp. 137–138.
2. Lawrence Lindman, "The Body Talks" *Penthouse*, March 1989.
3. Jake Tapper, *Body Slam* (New York: St. Martin's, 1999), p. 53.
4. Jessica Allen, *The Wit and Wisdom of Jesse "The Mind" Ventura* (New York: William Morrow, 1999), pp. 6–7.
5. Tapper, p. 53.

Chapter 6

1. Dan Cohen, *Wrestling Renegades* (New York: Pocket Books, 1999), pp. 15–16.
2. Cohen, pp. 27–28.
3. Jake Tapper, *Body Slam* (New York: St. Martin's, 1999), p. 64.

4. Captain Lou Albano, Bert Randolph Sugar, and Roger Woodson, *The Complete Idiot's Guide to Pro Wrestling* (New York: Alpha Books, 1999), p. 102.
5. Jesse Ventura, *I Ain't Got Time to Bleed* (New York: Villard, 1999), p. 115.
6. Tapper, p. 70.

Chapter 7
1. Jake Tapper, *Body Slam* (New York: St. Martin's, 1999), p. 78.
2. Jesse Ventura, *I Ain't Got Time to Bleed* (New York: Villard, 1999), p. 123.
3. Ventura, p. 127.
4. Dan Cohen, *Wrestling Renegades* (New York: Pocket Books, 1999), p. 20.

Chapter 8
1. Jake Tapper, *Body Slam* (New York: St. Martin's, 1999), pp. 102–103.
2. Tapper, p. 108.

Chapter 9
1. Jessica Allen, *The Wit and Wisdom of Jesse "The Mind" Ventura* (New York: William Morrow, 1999), pp. 30–31.
2. Jesse Ventura, *I Ain't Got Time to Bleed* (New York: Villard, 1999), p. 159.
3. Jake Tapper, *Body Slam* (New York: St. Martin's, 1999), p. 95.
4. Ventura, p. 173.
5. Ventura, p. 172.

Chapter 10
1. Jesse Ventura, *I Ain't Got Time to Bleed* (New York: Villard, 1999), p. 178.
2. Jake Tapper, *Body Slam* (New York; St. Martin's, 1999), p. 243.
3. Tapper, p. 242.

Books

Albano, Lou, and Bert Sugar. *The Complete Idiot's Guide to Pro Wrestling.* New York: Alpha Books, 1999.

Allen, Jessica. *The Wit and Wisdom of Jesse "The Mind" Ventura.* New York: William Morrow, 1999.

Cohen, Dan. *Wrestling Renegades.* New York: Archway Paperbacks, 1999.

Tapper, Jake. *Body Slam, The Jesse Ventura Story.* New York: St. Martin's Paperback, 1999.

Ventura, Jesse, with Julie Mooney. *Do I Stand Alone?* New York: Pocket Books, 2000.

Web Sites

The Jesse Ventura Volunteer Committee
   www.jesseventura.org
Office of Governor Jesse Ventura
   www.governor.state.mn.us/
The Ventura Files
   www.venturafiles.com